RULES OF THUMB

RULES OF THUMB

A LIFE MANUAL

BY TOM PARKER

WORKMAN PUBLISHING • NEW YORK

For Joy

Library of Congress Cataloging-in-Publication Data is available.

ISBN 978-0-7611-5073-2

Design by Janet Parker and Kate Lin
Photo editor: Anne Kerman

Workman books are available at special discounts when purchased in bulk for premiums and sales promotions as well as for fund-raising or educational use. Special editions or book excerpts can also be created to specification. For details, contact the Special Sales Director at the address below.

WORKMAN PUBLISHING COMPANY, INC.
225 Varick Street
New York, NY 10014-4381
www.workman.com

Printed in the United States of America

First printing October 2008
10 9 8 7 6 5 4 3 2

ACKNOWLEDGMENTS

Thanks to all those who have helped me with the Rules of Thumb project over the years and, more recently, on this new book. In particular I would like to thank Stewart Brand, who got me started; Kevin Kelly, Senior Maverick for *Wired* and the mind behind kk.org; Mark Frauenfelder of BoingBoing.com and *MAKE* magazine; my old pal Gerard Van der Leun of AmericanDigest.org; as well as Michael Rider, Kat Dalton, Cheryl Russell, Rick Eckstrom, Franklin Crawford, and the best day-to-day support team ever: Jamie, Dick, Kagan, and Connor Gehring.

Rulesofthumb.org is the centerpiece of this project. For that I would like to thank my wife and technical adviser, Joy Veronneau; Steve Carver of stevecarverdesign.com; and Zeeshan Arshad, who did prodigious amounts of software design and coding for the site. I would also like to thank the many Rules of Thumb contributors and the members of the Rulesofthumb.org Review Board. We are building a master list of Rules of Thumb contributors at rulesofthumb.org, so please join us.

A special thanks goes to Randall Lotowycz, Ruth Sullivan, Janet Parker, Kate Lin, Anne Kerman, and the other folks at Workman Publishing. Their vision for this book extended far beyond mine, and working with them has been a delight.

INTRODUCTION

Imagine this: You are driving on a busy freeway. A Lamborghini flies past you and then suddenly spins out of control. As your life flashes before your eyes, you remember:

Aim your vehicle for the spot where the car first spun out. At high speed, nothing stays in the same place for long. The car will have moved by the time you get there.

It works. You miss the Lamborghini by aiming for the spot where it lost control. A simple rule of thumb just saved your life and you look like an IndyCar all-star.

A rule of thumb is a homespun recipe for making a guess. It's an easy-to-remember guide that falls somewhere between a mathematical formula and a shot in the dark. A college student knows that, as a rule of thumb, 54 M&M's will give him the same jolt as two cups of coffee. A green-minded person knows that keeping a washable mug on her desk will save as many as 500 disposable/nondegradable cups a year. And an editor knows that if she really wants to get something done, she asks a busy person to do it.

These rules of thumb are mental tools to help you quickly appraise a situation or solve a problem. And sometimes they just make you look smart: Suppose you need to know the temperature outdoors but you don't have a thermometer. All you have to do is count the number of times a cricket chirps in 15 seconds and add 37. Bingo! You get a rough estimate of the temperature in degrees Fahrenheit.

I've been collecting rules of thumb for years, at first jotting them down in a notebook. After I published my initial collection, readers from all over the world sent me new rules. Some were written on fancy letterhead. Others arrived on napkins or stolen office stationery. One came scribbled on an airline barf bag! The writer Tom Wolfe sent a beautifully penned card with a rule of thumb about rental properties. The artist Robert Crumb sent his favorite rule in cartoon form. David Letterman had me on his show to read a selection of rules, and NPR shared many of their favorites on the air. Things sort of snowballed from there.

Eventually I needed a database to keep track of the rules, so I launched Rulesofthumb.org. The goal of the site is to gather every rule of thumb, submitted by thousands of clever users, into one easily searchable online reference database that will grow forever. All new rules must pass through a kind of Darwinian survival contest in which members vote them "in" or "out" and rate them on a scale of one to ten, based on how well they work. As the site has grown, we've added new, topical categories on subjects such as technology and green living. We even have a Rulesofthumb.org Review Board, which continually seeks out and evaluates rules of thumb from around the globe.

In *Rules of Thumb*, we've compiled the best tried-and-true rules, as well as the newest and most highly rated ones. This is not so much a book of facts as it is a book of experience. It's a collection of observations by people who bother to look at how things work and at how they get things done. Each rule is credited to the person who submitted it, although it's not necessarily that person's own invention—he or she simply liked it and wanted to pass it on. This generous offering of rules covers just about every subject imaginable—money, relationships, cooking, health, weather, cars, children, exercise, gardening, travel, restaurants, home—and is presented in random order for your reading pleasure. But if you want to look up a particular subject, we've included a handy index where everything is cross-referenced.

A hundred years ago, people used rules of thumb to make up for a lack of information. Today the problem is too *much* information (think having to wade through a gazillion hits on a Google search). Information overload makes the simple, memorable advice in *Rules of Thumb* more valuable than ever. The collected wisdom of the ages for those who like to guess with precision, this book is a shortcut to the fast lane for busy people like you. With it you can take the information you have and turn it into the information you need.

THE
RULES

weather and temperature

THE FAMOUS RED SUN RULE

Red sun at night, sailor's delight; red sun in the morning, sailor take warning.

—Isabel T. Coburn

style and appearance

SPORTING A HAT

Never wear a hat that has more character than you do.

—Michael Harris, hatmaker

cooking and entertaining

Hymn and Eggs

The song "Onward, Christian Soldiers" sung in a not-too-brisk tempo makes a good egg timer. If you put the egg into boiling water and sing all five verses, with the chorus, the egg will be just right when you come to "Amen."

—Mrs. G. H. Moore, quoted in *The New Yorker*

green living

Treading Lightly

When trying to cut back on your carbon footprint, figure that 40 percent is caused by the energy you use directly—driving, heating water, etc.—and the remaining 60 percent comes from the goods and services you buy.

—Lory Peck

the arts

ODDS AT THE OSCARS

Never bet on a movie that didn't earn a Best Director nomination. And if a movie wins for Best Director, it'll almost definitely win for Best Picture.

—Pam Rahn, office Oscar pool winner

automobiles

THE TAO OF BEING STUCK

You can't always back out of what you drive forward into, but you can always drive forward out of what you backed into.

—W. Woodsman

money and finance

MAKING AN AUDIT WORTHWHILE

To make an audit worthwhile, the IRS must find $300 worth of additional income or erroneous deductions per hour of investigation.

—P. Douglas Combs

safety and survival

Four-Legged Search Parties

One trained dog equals 60 search-and-rescue workers.

—Charles Stoehr

children and child care

READING RIGHTS

Give your child a library card when he or she is able to write his or her full name.

—Norman Brenner

health and body

CAUGHT NAPPING An hour's nap in the middle of the day equals three hours of sleep at night.

—Rulesofthumb.org Review Board

sports and recreation

SIZING A BASEBALL BAT

The length of a bat in inches shouldn't exceed its weight in ounces by more than two.

—Bill Carrier, coach

writing and presentation

Poetry Rhymes with Austerity

When writing a poem, eliminate nine out of ten adjectives and adverbs in the first draft, and cut everything you've heard before.

—Jennifer Welch, poet and editor

career and work life

BRANDING YOURSELF

Every time you do something wrong, your boss will remember it as three times that number. If the total number of actual mess-ups is greater than three, your boss will remember it as "always."

—Evan Christensen, unemployed

conversation and body language

Pausing to "Think"

When asked an important question, always pause for at least a silent count of three before answering. You will appear to be more thoughtful and intelligent.

—Rulesofthumb.org Review Board

education and school

SLEEPING IN TONGUES

You know you've become comfortable with a foreign language when you dream in that language.

—Dennis Palaganas

math and measurements

A QUARTER MEASURE

A U.S. quarter is just under one inch in width.

—Kate Gladstone

joker

ACADEMIA NUTS

Inviting more than 25 percent of the guests from the economics department to a university party ruins the conversation.

—Martha Farnsworth Riche,
former director of the U.S. Census Bureau

politics

BECOMING A HOUSEHOLD NAME

You need to run a TV ad at least 12 times if you want voters to remember your candidate.

—Jim Margolis,
political ad
specialist

business and sales

THE COST OF FREE HELP

You generally need three volunteers to make a training session worthwhile. If you have just one volunteer, you will save time if you skip the training and do the work yourself.

—Rulesofthumb.org Review Board

hobbies

THE ANTIQUES RULE OF THREE

Don't buy a piece of antique furniture if you can find three things wrong with it.

—Adam Perl, antiques dealer

computers and technology

A HOP, CLICK, AND JUMP AWAY

A well-designed website should let you navigate from one page to another in three clicks or less.

—Jessica Hines, web designer

gambling

Bankrolling Your Game

Don't enter a poker game unless you have 60 times the betting limit in your pocket.

—John Scarne, gambling authority

style and appearance

LEAVING NO ROOM FOR IMAGINATION Buy
the smallest swimsuit you can squeeze
yourself into; the life of a suit is inversely
proportional to its size.

—Kim Kohler-Lovejoy, fashionista

joker

A Genuine Haunting

You can determine whether a ghost is real by crossing your eyes. If the image doubles, the ghost is there. If not, it's all in your mind.

—Scott Parker, data specialist

green living

BRING-YOUR-MUG-TO-WORK DAY

Keeping a washable mug at your desk can save as many as 500 disposable paper or plastic cups a year.

—Rulesofthumb.org Review Board

pets

CHOOSING A CALM PUPPY

Pick a puppy whose tail wags in sync with its walk.

—Neil Schwartzbach

sports and recreation

RUBBERS GONE WILD

Always include condoms in your camping gear. They are great for protecting wristwatches, safeguarding money, and many other things.

—Denis Smith, high school counselor

safety and survival

SHOCKING ADVICE

Volts hurt; amps kill.

—Waldo Weyeris, engineer

wild card

PLANNING A MASSAGE

As a masseuse, you can expect a full-body massage to take 90 minutes, plus an additional 5 minutes for each bad joke the client makes before the session. The number of bad jokes is directly proportional to the thickness of a person's body armor.

—Geanne Toma, massage therapist

recreational vehicles

FULL OF HOT AIR

You get about half an hour of flight in a hot air balloon per 20-pound tank of propane gas.

—Barbara Frederking, balloonist

science

DISCOVERING A LOST CIVILIZATION

You won't unearth prehistoric archaeological finds on slopes greater than 20 percent (nine degrees).

—Thomas W. Neumann, anthropological archaeologist and wildlife ecologist

style and appearance

Choosing a Barber

Between two barbers in a shop, choose the one with the worse haircut; barbers cut each other's hair.

—George Cameron

relationships and romance

PRACTICING SAFE SEX Never sleep with anyone who's crazier than you are.

—Rulesofthumb.org Review Board

the arts

Staging a Modest Play

Squint while examining your stage. If any prop or color pops out, tone it down.

—Dean Sheridan, electronics technician and deaf actor

house and home

PICTURE PERFECT

Hang artwork so that the middle of the piece is at least 60 inches above the floor but never more than 10 inches above the furniture below it.

—Joseph Bauer, master carpenter

business and sales

THE GO-TO GUY

If you really need something done, ask a busy person.

—Ruth Sullivan, editor

weather and temperature

QUICK TEMPERATURE CONVERSION

To roughly convert Celsius to Fahrenheit, double the temperature and add 30. Thus 10°C is 50°F and 20°C is 70°F.

—Stephen J. Lambrechts-Forester

money and finance

AFFORDING A MORTGAGE

If you're responsible and hold a steady job, you should be able to support a mortgage that is three times your annual income.

—Jim Colby

sports and recreation

Sinking a Birdie

All putts break toward the water, even on greens that appear perfectly flat. That's because all greens are contoured for drainage.

—Donald B. Lilley, water tester

health and body

SAVING FACE

A person is seriously ill or injured if he suddenly falls forward without putting his hands up to protect his face.

—Gerry M. Flick, ship's surgeon

construction and architecture

EASY STREETS

A city street is most visually appealing if its width is the height of the buildings along its sides.

—David and Penny Russell

travel

Canned Memories

Snapshots encourage memories, videos replace them. After watching a video of your vacation, your memory of the vacation will be of what you saw on the video.

—Rulesofthumb.org Review Board

food and drink

Going for the Tart

If you like your Granny Smith apples extra tart, choose the ones with pale speckles and red patches.

—James Turner

green living

HARVESTING ETHANOL

One ton of corn will make about 50 gallons of ethanol, which has the energy content of 33 gallons of gasoline.

—Bob Horton, statistics consultant

safety and survival

FOOLING A MAD OSTRICH

If an enraged ostrich attacks you, lie down and pretend to be dead. It will think it has won and forget the whole episode within a few seconds, allowing you to retreat intact.

—Adrian Rinehart-Balfe

business and sales

SELLING WITH CHUTZPAH You can't sell something if it doesn't excite you.

—Rulesofthumb.org Review Board

hobbies

Pricing Your Handiwork

To price a sweater or similar piece of knitted handiwork, multiply the cost of your materials by three. The resulting figure should represent a reasonable hourly wage, while keeping the price affordable.

—Carol Terrizzi, artist and graphic designer

safety and survival

CAUTIOUS DRIVING

You should keep at least one car length between your car and the car ahead for every ten miles per hour of speed.

—Carla Corin

joker

A BUS RIDE TO CRAZYTOWN

To avoid lunatics on city buses, sit in the middle. The friendly lunatics sit as close to the driver as they can, and the unfriendly ones sit as far away as they can.

—Keith Allan Hunter

children and child care

THE BEST OF THE BUNCH

Dress the best-behaved child first, because he or she is less likely to undo your preparations by the time you're ready to leave.

—L. Musselman, mother

wild card

CHEWING ON A PEARL

To tell if a pearl is genuine, rub it against your teeth. A fake pearl will feel smooth; the real thing will grate.

—Quinith Janssen, pearl expert

construction and architecture

Taking a Rain Check

When raindrops hit your windshield faster than you can count them, it's time to knock off work for the day.

—Gene Beitel, contractor

house and home

Eek! A Mouse!

If you think you saw a mouse, you did.

—Rulesofthumb.org Review Board

business and sales

DUCKING A MEETING

A meeting is not worth attending if the trip takes more time than the duration of the meeting itself.

—David Liddle, pastor

advertising and design

The "Free" in Freelancing

Graphic artists and designers should expect to put in one unbillable hour for every billable one. The unpaid time will be spent doing promotional work and dealing with difficult customers.

—Michael Rider, graphic designer and art director

sports and recreation
POOL TABLE TACTICS
In a game of eight-ball, let your opponent sink half his balls before you sink your first. That way, your balls will interfere with his shooting, not the other way around.

—John Lilly, mechanical engineer and cliff diver

food and drink
RACKING UP YEARS
When cellaring a wine, add about one year of aging time for every 2 degrees the cellar averages below 65 degrees Fahrenheit.

—Craig Goldwyn, wine writer

health and body
RECOVERY TIME
For every day you spend in the hospital, plan on one week to recuperate.

—Jon Crispin

wild card

PHOTO-SHARING ETIQUETTE If you're showing slides or photos to company you went on vacation with, show only half the pictures. If your company wasn't there, show only one out of five—and then only if you're asked.

—Frank Cleary, teacher and physicist

computers and technology

THE FIRST RULE OF COMPUTER SUPPORT

When asking someone if his or her computer is turned on, specify that you are not talking about the monitor.

—Tony Casazza

conversation and body language

FABULOUS FIBBING

When lying, don't explain too much. And remember that odd numbers are more believable than even numbers.

—Terry Larimore, therapist

joker

The Bathroom Reading Rule

If you read on the john every morning, it'll take you six weeks to finish the book.

—Gaard Moses

green living

The Green Mileage

At highway speeds, using the A/C is more gas efficient than leaving the windows open, which greatly increases wind drag on your car.

—Jimmy Mintern, auto technician

fitness and exercise

STAND UP TO BACK PAIN

If your back hurts more when you climb stairs, walk up a hill, or get out of a chair, you need to do extension exercises.

—Peggy Bodine-Reese, physical therapist

sports and recreation

CHOOSING YOUR QUIVER

To estimate the arrow length that's best for you, hold the end of a yardstick against your breastbone with your hands together and extended in front of you. The best length is where your fingertips touch the yardstick.

—Dana Burdick

business and sales

HAND-OFF MANAGEMENT

If you are in a position to do so, delegate a task to someone else if he or she can do it 80 percent as well as you would. This will leave you time to do the things that only you can do.

—Elliot Miller

the arts

TRACKING BOOK SALES

If a publisher says it's too soon to tell if a book is selling well, it isn't.

—Walter Pitkin, literary agent

recreational vehicles

BICYCLE TRAVEL

On a good highway bicycle you can travel 50 miles per day at a leisurely pace.

—Alwyn T. Perrin, editor of *Explorers Ltd. Source Book*

safety and survival

AVOIDING TORNADOES Never try to outrace a tornado when you're driving. Instead, drive perpendicular to its direction of travel.

—Rulesofthumb.org Review Board

hobbies

WATERING YOUR GARDEN

Don't water your garden unless the soil is dry past the depth of your index finger.

—Cally Arthur, editor and communications coordinator

career and work life

QUICK RESPONSES

During a job interview, try to answer every question in 60 seconds or less.

—Cheryl A. Russell, editorial director of *New Strategist Publications*

politics

Rule of Political Interests

If a politician mentions "special interests," he or she is discussing someone or some group with whom he or she disagrees. On the contrary, the "public interest" is always something with which he or she is in complete agreement.

—Bill Bacon, web manager

food and drink

Recreational Poppy Seed Use

One poppy seed bagel or muffin can register a positive for opiates on a drug test for up to 48 hours after the food was eaten.

—Rulesofthumb.org Review Board

wild card

PAINTING A HIGHWAY

A road must carry traffic of at least 400 cars per day for a reflective centerline to be a cost-effective improvement.

—John Schubert, senior editor

style and appearance

LOOKING GOOD ON TV

You will look more alert on TV if you lean forward.

—Sharon K. Yntema, writer

animals and wildlife
PISSED-OFF LIONS
Don't stand within 16 feet of the lion tunnel when the lions are entering or exiting the ring. They will pee on you.

—Todd Strong, circus school student

construction and architecture
CHARMING PITCH
When you are planning a house, make the angle of the roof noticeably more or noticeably less than a right angle; otherwise, the appearance lacks charm and is curiously depressing. In general, the steeper the roof, the more charm the house will have.

—Susan Pitkin, librarian

house and home
Going off Half Caulked
You need one cartridge of caulk for every two windows or doors.

—James T. Dulley

safety and survival

THE SURVIVAL RULE OF THREE

You can live 3 seconds without blood, 3 minutes without air, 3 days without water, and 3 weeks without food.

—Sandy Figuers, geologist

pets

RUBBED THE WRONG WAY

Rub a horse's face and ears as gently as you would pet a cat.

—Stacey DiGiovani, equestrian

green living

Offsetting Heating Bills

Each degree you lower your thermostat during the winter will lower your overall heating bill by 3 percent.

—Jim Colby

automobiles

PAYING FOR THE WHOLE CAR Never sign up for car payments that are more than 10 percent of your monthly income.

—Rulesofthumb.org Review Board

wild card

Telling the Irish from the Scots

A surname starting with "Mc" is more likely to be Irish; one starting with "Mac" is more likely to be Scottish.

—Rulesofthumb.org Review Board

health and body

WAITING TO EXHALE

A healthy adult should be able to completely exhale a deep breath in three seconds.

—Dr. James Macmillan

joker

ANNOYING A MUSICIAN

The most frequent and annoying song request for piano players is "Piano Man." For guitarists, it's "Stairway to Heaven." For drummers, "Wipe Out." For singer/rhythm guitarists, "Free Bird." For fiddlers, "The Devil Went Down to Georgia." And for sax players, the intro to "Baker Street."

—Psachya Septimus, musician

sports and recreation

Control Center

If you can control the center of a chessboard early, you control the game.

—Rulesofthumb.org Review Board

children and child care

Taste Test for Tots

If your baby tastes extremely salty when you kiss him or her, speak with your doctor about testing for cystic fibrosis.

—Dr. Tom Ferguson,
editor of *Medical Self-Care*

cooking and entertaining

TELL TAIL LOBSTERS

If a boiled lobster's tail isn't curled, it was dead before it was boiled.

—T. M. Prudden,
lobster expert

health and body

FAT FLOATS

If your turds float, there's too much fat in your diet.

—Rulesofthumb.org Review Board

house and home

Choosing a Chandelier

The diagonal dimension of a chandelier in inches should equal the diagonal dimension of the dining room in feet. Also, the diameter of the chandelier should be at least 12 inches less than the diameter of the dining room table.

—from the American Home Lighting Institute

food and drink

RESERVATIONS ABOUT THE HELP

Don't go to a restaurant that has a sign in the window advertising for waiters. It's hard enough to get waited on in a restaurant that thinks it has plenty of help.

—Andy Rooney, television commentator

conversation and body language

Quieting a Drunk

The easiest way to quiet a drunk is to whisper to him.

—Rulesofthumb.org Review Board

money and finance

DOUBLING YOUR MONEY

The amount of time for an investment to double is roughly equal to 72 divided by the annualized interest rate.

—Nathan Odle, real estate developer and civil engineer

safety and survival

BACKING UP AN ARMY

Each soldier on the front lines requires ten support personnel in the rear.

—Elliot Miller

house and home

SCHEDULING A GARAGE SALE The big spenders never come before noon.

—Rulesofthumb.org Review Board

Stopping the Sting

Use ammonia for a bee sting and vinegar for a wasp sting.

—Dr. Bill Grierson, professor emeritus at the
University of Florida

hobbies

HANDSOME HANDWRITING

The most pleasing height for lowercase italic letters is five times the width of the pen point, or nib.

—Ashley Miller, calligrapher

business and sales

EXPENSE ACCOUNTING

Don't buy a new piece of equipment for your business unless it can pay for itself in three months.

—Kevin Kelly, writer and technologist

wild card

PROPERLY HOARDING MAGAZINES

To prevent a stack of magazines from falling over, change the direction of the binding every sixth issue.

—Dennis Palaganas

computers and technology

Buying an Extended Warranty

The extended warranty is never worth buying on a watch, rarely worth buying on a stereo or video component, sometimes worth buying on a TV or desktop computer, and always worth buying on a laptop computer.

—Mark H. Anbinder,
tech writer and Apple guru

food and drink

SMART DINING

If the price of the veal is equal to or only slightly more than the price of the chicken, order the chicken.

—Len Coloccia

animals and wildlife

The Scoop on Scat

Wild feline scat, such as that of panthers and bobcats, dries from the inside out. If a pile of cat poop still looks wet, don't assume it is fresh.

—Rulesofthumb.org Review Board

joker

AIRBAGS AND WINDBAGS

The person doing the most talking after a fender bender is usually the one who caused the accident.

—Steve Carver

cooking and entertaining

MAKING A PERFECT MERINGUE

Stop beating egg whites when they lose their shine and you'll have the perfect meringue.

—Jeffrey Buben, chef

conversation and body language

CONVERTING ENEMIES If you can make people who are dead set against you laugh, that's the first step to winning them over to your side.

—attributed to John Waters, filmmaker

green living

SNUGGING UP A HOUSE

A superinsulated house (i.e., one with larger amounts of insulation, airtight construction, and controlled ventilation) should have 12 square feet of windows for every 100 square feet of floor. And at least two thirds of the windows should be facing south.

—Phillip Close, builder

recreational vehicles

SIZING A CANOE PADDLE

Stand the canoe paddle on the ground in front of you. The handle should reach your chin if you plan to paddle from the bow; it should reach your eyes if you are paddling from the stern.

—Peter van Berkum

travel

HITCH-HIKING IN AFRICA

Allow one week to hitchhike a thousand kilometers in Africa.

—Henning Pape

pets

Managing Litter Boxes

You should have one litter box per cat plus one.

—Rulesofthumb.org Review Board

automobiles

CAR TALK

If your engine knocks during acceleration, it's probably the connecting rod. If the engine knocks during deceleration, it's probably the piston wrist pin. If you have piston slap (too much room between the piston and the cylinder wall), the knock will be loudest when the engine is cold and idling.

—Ray Hill, car-care columnist

weather and temperature

TELLTALE BREATH

When you can see your breath, the temperature is below 45 degrees Fahrenheit.

—Thomas Lack

animals and wildlife
IDENTIFYING GEESE

If geese are in a close V formation, they are almost certainly Canada geese. If they form a looser V that's rippling or are in a long diagonal line, they are probably the less common snow geese.

—Hal Borland, author and journalist

the arts
WRITING A SCREENPLAY

One page of an average screenplay equals about one minute of screen time. Therefore, the script for a typical feature film should be about a hundred pages long. In fact, many studios and producers won't look at screenplays that are much longer.

—John Griesemer, writer and actor

style and appearance
Shaving by the Clock

Your face is usually dry and puffy when you first wake up. For each hour you slept, put off shaving for two minutes.

—E. L. Beck

food and drink

STOCKPILING THE HARD STUFF

The harder the cheese, the longer it will keep.

—Rulesofthumb.org Review Board

pets

BEST OF CLASS

The more nervous you are while showing your dog, the more nervous your dog will be.

—Kari Casher,
dog breeder

advertising and design

LONG-DISTANCE READING

To determine the readable distance, in feet, of words on a billboard, take half the height of one of the letters in inches and multiply by 100.

—Thos. Hodgson, Hodgson Signs

house and home

BUYING OCEANSIDE PROPERTY If you are
north of the equator, don't buy property
on the south side of a jetty. The drift of
the ocean is from south to north, and the
beach will erode any southern protrusion.

—Carol Terrizzi, artist and graphic designer

writing and presentation

SPEAKING WITH CLARITY

When writing a speech, never include a word you have to look up.

—Rulesofthumb.org Review Board

relationships and romance

Getting Thoroughly Acquainted

It takes 30 hours of conversation to know whether you really like someone. Be wary of anyone who invites you only to places where you can't chat, such as movies, plays, or concerts.

—B. Bell

health and body

BODY COUNT

To estimate the surface area of your body, multiply the surface area of your palm by 100. And to estimate the weight of your skin, divide your body weight by 16.

—Scott M. Kruse, biogeographer

business and sales

Palatable Criticism

In a performance review, don't offer more than three criticisms. That's all an employee can digest.

—Nancy Humphries, personnel consultant

food and drink

SLAUGHTERHOUSE FOUR

A properly butchered beef carcass is one quarter steaks, a quarter ground beef and stew meat, a quarter roasts, and a quarter waste.

—Harry Pound, Pound's Meat Cutting

green living

DROPPING CHARGES

In most cases, a lithium battery will last as long as four alkaline batteries, and an alkaline battery will last as long as ten carbon-zinc batteries.

—W. Price

safety and survival

GASPING FOR HELP

If a choking person can verbally request the Heimlich maneuver, he or she doesn't need it.

—Dr. James Macmillan

law and crime

A POORLY FITTING SUIT

If your lawyer tells you that the prospective lawsuit is a "slam dunk," retain a new lawyer as soon as possible.

—Stephen Verbit, attorney

relationships and romance

NEVER GO TO BED MAD

To stay married, patch up your arguments before you go to bed.

—Rulesofthumb.org Review Board

pets

CANINE ETIQUETTE When guests bring a dog along, always serve your dog before theirs.

—Cheryl A. Russell,
editorial director of *New Strategist Publications*

wild card

LOGGING LAUNDROMAT TIME

Plan on spending 90 minutes at the Laundromat. If you go on a weekend after 8 A.M., or on a weekday after 5:30 P.M., add 15 minutes per load to your time estimate.

—Joe Rappaport, Straphangers campaign coordinator

cooking and entertaining

Flawless Fillets

Cook fish ten minutes per inch of thickness.

—Rulesofthumb.org Review Board

children and child care

A SPOONFUL OF DINNER

Children don't need huge servings of food. Start with one tablespoon of each item per year of age.

—Gayle Peterson, mother

house and home

Burglarproofing Your House

The next time you come home, pretend you don't have your keys. The way you get in your house is the way a burglar will, too.

—Rulesofthumb.org Review Board

sports and recreation

GET A GRIP

To choose the right grip for a tennis racket, measure the distance from the tip of your middle finger to the crease in the middle of your palm; that equals the right-size handle.

—Dr. David Bachman

food and drink

MAKING WINE

One ton of grapes will make 170 gallons of wine.

—L. Wagner, vintner

health and body

CRACKING YOUR KNUCKLES

You have to wait 30 minutes after cracking your knuckles to crack them again. That's how long it takes for the vaporized joint fluid to go back into solution.

—Jim Crissman, veterinary pathologist

the arts

AMASSING A MUSIC COLLECTION

You will not tire of your personal music library if you have 200 or more CDs of various genres.

—Rusty Cartmill

law and crime

PREDICTING A VERDICT

A returning jury that avoids looking at the defendant has convicted him.

—Rulesofthumb.org Review Board

writing and presentation

WRAPPING UP YOUR RESEARCH

You're done with your research when those you interview urge you to interview people you've already interviewed.

—Robert Kanigel

automobiles

A FISTFUL OF DAMAGE

Exterior damage the size of your hand equals about one hour's work.

—Rulesofthumb.org Review Board

career and work life

Background Check

When you are checking a reference and ask someone's former employer whether he or she would hire the person again, any answer but "yes" is a "no."

—Edward J. Garrison, nursing home administrator

recreational vehicles

BICYCLES BUILT FOR TWO Expect a tandem bicycle to be about 20 percent faster than a single bike.

—John Schubert, senior editor

politics

Grassroots Math

For every person who gets involved in your campaign by contributing money, putting up a lawn sign, distributing literature, or signing an endorsement letter, expect 10 to 15 votes on election day.

—Tom Wilbur, county commissioner

math and measurements

THE RULE OF NINE

The product of anything multiplied by nine will have digits that add up to nine or to a number divisible by nine.

—Rulesofthumb.org Review Board

hobbies

GROWING PLANTS INDOORS

For every square foot of growing area, you need at least 20 watts of fluorescent light.

—Amy Rice

construction and architecture

BUILDING AN IGLOO

An igloo should be built in an area where the snow is packed just loose enough for you to make a footprint, but not so loose that the footprint disappears in a high wind.

—Dennis Eskow, science editor for *Popular Mechanics*

house and home

SPEED-PAINTING WINDOWS

It's faster to get paint on the glass and remove it afterward than it is to mask all the edges.

—Maitlen W. Montmarency, painter

health and body

KNOWING WHEN YOUR TIME IS UP

If you can hear a "code blue" in the hospital, it's not for you.

—Rulesofthumb.org Review Board

green living

IDLE MOMENTS

Turn off your engine if it will be idling for more than one minute.

—Owen Chambers, petroleum distributor

style and appearance

THE ANN LANDERS PENCIL TEST

To determine whether you need to wear a bra, place a pencil under one of your breasts. If the pencil falls to the floor, you don't need to wear a bra; if it stays, you need one.

—Ann Landers, advice columnist

science

Preventing a Chemistry Mishap

Choose a flask that has at least twice the capacity of the liquid you want to put in it.

—Frank Cleary, teacher and physicist

travel

PASSING THE BAR If the bar at your hotel is well laid out and well stocked, and the bartender is able to be both professional and friendly, you can look forward to your stay.

—John Bodoni

joker

The High Cost of Living

Time goes by faster from the moment one starts paying one's own bills.

—Franklin Crawford, writer

education and school

SPOTTING A GOOD TEACHER

You know you're presenting a well-crafted lesson if a student can walk into the lecture ten minutes late and catch up on most of the material he or she missed.

—Rulesofthumb.org Review Board

sports and recreation

A COLD DAY IN THE PARK

A Frisbee will crack and break when you can see your breath.

—Grady Wells, editor

sports and recreation

HUNTING FOR DEER

The vital target area on a white-tailed deer is about the size of a paper plate. Never shoot from farther away than you can consistently hit a paper plate.

—Dr. Timothy Haywood

cooking and entertaining

MOTHER OF ALL OMELETS

One ostrich egg will serve 24 people for brunch.

—from *The Joy of Cooking*

wild card

Making a Name in Mathematics

If you haven't made an important discovery in the field of mathematics by the time you're 22, you probably never will.

—Gerald Gutlipp, mathematician

health and body

STRESS TEST

Warm hands indicate relaxation. Cool hands indicate tension.

—Jan Lowenstein, writer

writing and presentation

TRIPLE THE EFFORT

You need to make your key points three times if you expect your audience to remember them.

—Rulesofthumb.org Review Board

recreational vehicles

STANDING TOO CLOSE TO A HELICOPTER

The dangerous gale-force rotor wash of a hovering helicopter extends outward to a distance three times the diameter of the main rotor.

—David A. Shugarts, editor for *Aviation Safety*

When Outer Space Comes Knocking

To determine the size of a meteorite, divide the diameter of its crater by 20.

—Rulesofthumb.org Review Board

travel
HEAD ROOM

On a Greyhound bus, the side with the toilet has more legroom than the side with the driver.

—Neil Hess, ski instructor

food and drink
CURBING YOUR DOGS

Throw out hot dogs when the liquid in the package becomes cloudy.

—Zak Mettgar, writer and vegetarian

animals and wildlife

GIANT SNAKE WRANGLING When handling pythons, anacondas, boas, and other large constrictors, it's wise to have one person for every four or five feet of snake.

—Donald R. Gentner

computers and technology

CHOOSING A DIGITAL CAMERA

A 6 megapixel (MP) digital camera is good for snapshots, web publishing, and 8" × 10" prints, and is even adequate for 16" × 20" prints. For 20" × 30" posters and full-page magazine photography, 10 MP would be better. However, a top-notch 6 MP camera takes better pictures than a cheapo 10 MP camera. Dollar for dollar, quality trumps megapixels.

—Mark H. Anbinder, tech writer and Apple guru

automobiles

Vintage vs. Just Old

Never buy a silver car. They rust sooner than others.

—Skip Eisiminger

weather and temperature

WHEN THE ANTS GO MARCHING

When ants travel in a straight line, expect rain. When they scatter, expect fair weather.

—Rulesofthumb.org Review Board

gambling

HARNESSING A WINNER

It's usually safe to bet on a horse that has just been assigned a leading full-time jockey. The trainer believes the horse is ready to win.

—Don Valliere, track manager and author

house and home

CHRISTMAS TREE RULE OF THREE

To find out how many old-fashioned lights your Christmas tree needs, multiply the tree height times the tree width times three.

—Michael Spencer, lawyer

sports and recreation

Tactical Tiles

A moderately experienced Scrabble player should average at least 20 points per word.

—C(3)H(4)R(1)I(1)S(1)T(1)Y(4), Scrabble nut

business and sales

Breaking in Clients

Expect a job with a new client to take about 25 percent longer than the same job would with an established client.

—Rulesofthumb.org Review Board

safety and survival

WEARING NO PANTS

On a cold day, wearing soaking-wet blue jeans will draw heat from your lower body twice as quickly as wearing no pants at all.

—Rob Weinberg

hobbies

BONSAI MAINTENANCE

If it takes more than one minute for the water to drain from your bonsai pot, it's time to repot. Proper bonsai culture requires rapid drainage through fresh and sandy soil.

—Rick Eckstrom, structural engineer

relationships and romance

ANNOYING HABITS If your fiancé does something that bothers you before you're married, it will bother you ten times more after you're married.

—Bruno Colapietro, matrimonial lawyer

conversation and body language

POWDER ROOM RULES

It takes four teenage girls to accompany one to the bathroom. Young adults go in threes, and older women go in pairs.

—Phillip Williams Jr.

advertising and design

WRITING SNAPPY COPY

To determine which words sparkle and which are duds in your ad copy, read it backward.

—Timothy Wenk, magician

sports and recreation

PLAYING CATCH

To catch a ball without a glove, the ends of your pinkie fingers should touch if the ball is coming at you below the waist. The ends of your thumbs should touch if the ball is coming in above your waist.

—Rulesofthumb.org Review Board

green living
THINK INK

For most print jobs at work, the "draft" option, which generates lighter printouts, is suitable. You'll use less toner and extend the cartridge life.

—Jack Romig,
green writer

construction and architecture
ADOBE DOs

The height of an adobe wall should be less than ten times its thickness unless it is stiffened by buttresses or intersecting partitions.

—Marcia Southwick, writer and builder

gambling
Getting to 21

When you're playing blackjack, assume that any unseen card is an eight.

—Rulesofthumb.org Review Board

writing and presentation

Eliminating Semicolons

You can replace about two thirds of the semicolons in most writing with a period. The rest of the time, you need a conjunction.

—Don Marti, editor

joker

GETTING DOWN TO BUSINESS

The more time you spend on foreplay, the less time you have afterward to make a really good snack.

—Johnny Carson

the arts

CRITIC-PROOF FILMS

If a movie is released without having any press screenings, it's probably a stinker.

—Rulesofthumb.org Review Board

children and child care

PLAYGROUND SAFETY

If playground monitors are close enough to have a normal conversation, they are too close together to adequately supervise children and need to spread out.

—Paul Beard

conversation and body language

SERVING TIME AT DINNER

A dinner guest who has recently been released from jail will reach for his spoon first regardless of what is being served.

—Rulesofthumb.org Review Board

style and appearance

FLEETING BEAUTY

People who wear their hair short will generally need a haircut within a week after their hair looks perfect.

—Ann Kimbrough

health and body

EATING LIKE A THIN PERSON Before you eat, ask yourself how hungry you are on a scale from 1 to 10, with 1 being an empty stomach and 10 the stuffed, bloated, after-Thanksgiving-dinner feeling. Eat only when you rate your hunger a 1 or 2. Then stop when you reach 5.

—Evette M. Hackman, R.D., Ph.D., consulting nutritionist

cooking and entertaining

SIGNATURE CHOCOLATE

Your hot fudge is ready when you can write your name on the surface with a spoon without the letters disappearing before you finish writing.

—Robin Masson

wild card

THE RANCHER'S RULE

Always leave a gate the way you found it.

—Merritt Holloway, Deep Springs Ranch

hobbies

Planting a Bulb

If you're not sure how deep to plant a flower bulb, try three times its length.

—Rulesofthumb.org Review Board

house and home

Low Overhead

There is cause for concern if the ridge of a house sags more than half an inch per year. Call an expert.

—Albert Snyder

law and crime

NABBING BANK ROBBERS

Bank robbers escaping by car will more often turn right than left because they don't want to waste valuable time waiting for cross traffic to clear.

—Paul LaVasseur,
police officer

business and sales

OPENING UP TO YOUR STAFF

If you have to call a meeting to tell everyone that you have an open-door policy, you have already failed as a manager.

—Rulesofthumb.org Review Board

money and finance

BUYING AN ENGAGEMENT RING

Plan on spending three months' salary on an engagement ring.

—Rulesofthumb.org Review Board

sports and recreation

The Skinny on Skinny

An ideal weight for an endurance athlete, in pounds, is twice his or her height in inches. That's about as lean and mean as many people would *like* to be in their marathon fantasies.

—Ned Frederick, writer

math and measurements

AN EAR FOR SPEED

To estimate the speed of a train in miles per hour, count the number of clicks in 29 seconds.

—Don Dalley

writing and presentation

Character Trumps Plot

Always figure out your characters before you figure out your plot. You can follow a good character through a bad plot, but you can't make a plot good with a bad character.

—Rulesofthumb.org Review Board

automobiles

CAR COMMITMENT

To get the best value from a car, buy it used and keep it for ten years.

—Dennis Pollack, contractor

safety and survival

EXPLORING A CAVE

Always have at least four people for any caving expedition. If someone is injured, two people can go for help while one stays with the injured spelunker. That way, no one is alone in the cave.

—David McClurg, speleologist

business and sales

SELLING TO THE ELDERLY For marketing purposes, assume that elderly consumers think they are 15 years younger than they actually are.

—Tracy Lux Frances

green living

Heating a Greenhouse

Containers of water are excellent for storing heat in a solar greenhouse. Start with one cubic foot of water for each square foot of greenhouse glass.

—Janet Hopper

sports and recreation

BUBBLING UP TO THE SURFACE

When scuba diving, don't rise to the surface any faster than the smallest bubbles you exhale.

—Alex Stewart

math and measurements

REMEMBERING THE DAYS IN A MONTH

Clench your fists and put them beside each other, thumb to thumb and knuckles aligned. Going from left to right, each knuckle represents a month with 31 days and each valley represents one with 30 days or fewer.

—Rulesofthumb.org Review Board

hobbies

THE JAPANESE RULE OF FLOWER ARRANGING

Put one third as many flowers as you think you need into the vase, then take half of them out.

—Lewy Olfson

money and finance

LOADING UP ON LIFE INSURANCE

If you have young children, your life insurance should be five or six times your salary. If you don't have children, the amount should be enough to pay off your debt.

—Rulesofthumb.org Review Board

career and work life

Yuletide Yield

You can plan on eventually harvesting 400 to 500 Christmas trees for every 1,000 seedlings you plant.

—Jay Waring, plant specialist

sports and recreation

FLYING A KITE

If the wind is lifting loose paper off the ground and raising dust, it is too strong for the average kite.

—Tal Streeter, kite builder

joker

REVIEWING A MENU

If you find three or more typos in the menu, ask for bottled water; six or more, consume only that water; nine or more, take the menu home as a souvenir.

—A. Brador, professor

safety and survival

Have Bumper Sticker, Will Rage

Drivers who customize their cars with bumper stickers and other adornments are more prone to road rage than are others.

—Rulesofthumb.org Review Board

style and appearance

DRESSING FOR THE GYM Dress for comfort and a good range of movement. Don't worry about what others think of what you're wearing. They're too wrapped up in their own workout to notice—unless, of course, your private parts are hanging out.

—Rulesofthumb.org Review Board

fitness and exercise

GYM EXCUSE

If your symptoms are above the neck (stuffy nose, sneezing), it's okay to exercise. If your symptoms are below the neck (chest cough, muscle aches and pains, intestinal), it's best to skip it.

—Rulesofthumb.org Review Board

weather and temperature

Ice Hocking

When spit freezes before it hits the ground, it's at least 40 degrees below 0 Fahrenheit.

—Jeanie MacDonough

hobbies

A Rose of Any Other Size . . .

A flower arrangement should usually be about one and a half times the height or width of the container.

—Pamela Reeger, florist

health and body

THE SHINGLES RULE

If shingles (herpes zoster) is found on the tip of your nose, it's likely in your eye as well, and you should make an emergency visit to an ophthalmologist.

—J. Robert Franks, physician associate

cooking and entertaining

EXPECTING GUESTS

Plan for only half of those you invite to a large social gathering, such as a wedding or retirement party, to attend. But expect a 90 percent turnout if you're inviting a small, select group of friends or family.

—Rulesofthumb.org Review Board

the arts

THE STOLEN ART RULE

Fewer than one in five stolen paintings are ever found.

—Nick Watt, ABC news correspondent

conversation and body language

TALKING IN CHINESE

You need to know and understand 5,000 words and characters in Chinese before trying to have a meaningful conversation.

—Paul A. Delaney

education and school

Choosing a College Course

The quality of the professor is more important than the subject of the course.

—Rulesofthumb.org Review Board

house and home

BAGGING THE YARD WORK

If you mow your lawn regularly and cut no more than one third of the length of the grass, you can safely leave the clippings on the lawn.

—R. A. Heindl

construction and architecture

Paving with Bricks

A crew of six bricklayers with one foreman can lay 1,000 square feet of paving brick per day.

—R. Pieper, architectural historian

cooking and entertaining

YEAST COMMON DENOMINATOR

To see whether your dough has risen enough, poke two holes into it the depth of the first joint of your thumb. If the holes are still there after 30 seconds, it has risen enough.

—Rulesofthumb.org Review Board

safety and survival

LAUNCHING FIREWORKS

When you're launching fireworks, make sure the audience stands five steps back for every ounce of propellant in the missile.

—Alan R. Reno

the arts

FORKING OUT FOR INSTRUMENTS If you're buying a musical instrument for a beginner, spend twice as much as you think you should. The instrument will be better built, sound better, and be easier to play. And it will have a better resale value.

—Jim Willett, musician

money and finance

SAVING FOR HOUSE REPAIRS

Homeowners should plan on reserving $100 a month for a home-repair fund. Total net costs for repairs per year can be 40 to 45 percent more than your base mortgage.

—Rulesofthumb.org Review Board

politics

DUCKING AN ELECTION-DAY FIASCO

When using touch-screen electronic voting machines, assume 2.5 minutes per voter and provide one machine for every 250 voters to prevent having long lines at your polling place.

—Doug Mabee, polling assistant

house and home

GARAGE SALE PRICING

To cover costs and show a profit, aim to triple your money on things that sell for less than $5 and double your money on things that sell for more than $5.

—Sam Gaben

advertising and design

PLANNING A TELEVISION AD

The visual component of a TV commercial accounts for 85 percent of its impact on the viewer; the sound track accounts for 15 percent.

—John Koten, staff reporter for
The Wall Street Journal

travel

A RIVER WINDS THROUGH IT

Under normal conditions, the distance that a river will run straight is never greater than ten times its width.

—Doug Knowles,
guitar maker

food and drink

Fooling Flavor Buds

When using shredded cheese in a recipe, you can substitute up to half fat-free cheese without hurting the flavor. The same is true for substituting fat-free or 2% milk for whole milk.

—Rulesofthumb.org Review Board

sports and recreation

Controlling a Baseball Pitch

The farther toward the fingertips you hold the ball, the faster the pitch; the closer you choke it in your hand, the slower the pitch.

—Ric Lessmann, head baseball coach

computers and technology

TESTING WEB BROWSERS

If you only have time to do thorough testing of your website in two web browsers, use Internet Explorer and Firefox. The website needs to work in Internet Explorer because so many people use it by default, and if it works in Firefox, it'll work in nearly all the other browsers.

—Mark H. Anbinder, tech writer and Apple guru

health and body

PACING THE DELIVERY

If a woman can walk around during contractions, she is not fully dilated.

—Dr. K. Emmott

house and home

THE MOVING RULE When moving to a new
home, set up your bed first. By the end
of the day you'll be glad to have a comfy
place in which to pass out.

—Jeremy Reid, graphic designer

wild card

BAD CREDIT

If your credit card can't be read when swiped at the cash register, wrap a clear or white plastic bag around it and try swiping it again. The bag covers up the scratches on the card's magnetic strip, allowing it to be read.

—Rulesofthumb.org Review Board

style and appearance

SPOTTING A BLINK

If you think you blinked during a photo, close your eyes and see what color spot you see. If the spot is white, you didn't blink. If the spot is red, you did. (Because the eyelid has many capillaries, they will render a red spot if the flash went through them.)

—John Zappulla

hobbies

GROWING HERBS

To plot your herb bed, figure two square feet for each variety you plan to grow.

—Jean Moses

joker

Blow It Out Your Nose

To get a good "blow" out of a stuffed-up nose, always blow the clearer nostril first.

—Joseph N. Tormos

fitness and exercise

EXERCISING FOR LIFE

For every hour that you're physically active, you can expect to live two hours longer.

—Robert H. Thomas, writer

pets

DISCIPLINING A DOG

If a dog misbehaves, you must correct the behavior within 1.5 seconds. Otherwise, the dog won't make the connection between what it did and your correction.

—James Erwin

money and finance

SELLING REAL ESTATE

Rental property should sell for about 100 times its monthly rental income.

—Tom Wolfe, writer

business and sales

AN OFFER YOU CAN'T REFUSE

Count on 10 to 15 percent of customers who accept a trial offer to return the merchandise. It's still better to provide a trial offer than a money-back guarantee because the former typically produces about twice as many orders.

—Jim Kobs, Kobs and Brady Advertising

food and drink

Not So Hot Potato

You should never order a baked potato near closing time.

—C. A. Fuller, EMT

weather and temperature

FRUITFUL ADVICE

Tough apple skin means a hard winter.

—Rulesofthumb.org Review Board

---

children and child care

KEEPING AN EYE ON TROUBLE-MAKERS

The first thing to check about a disruptive elementary student is his or her eyesight.

—Steven M. Keisman, high school resource coordinator

business and sales

A SOFT SELL

A new computer hardware product will start to sell two to three months sooner than a new software product. That's because hardware is built to solve obvious needs, like lack of memory. Software is designed to solve less obvious needs, and users don't buy until they read a product review.

—Ben Cota, technology marketing guy

animals and wildlife

DRIVING IN A FOREIGN COUNTRY Slow down
for donkeys, speed up for goats, and stop
for cows. Donkeys will get out of your way,
it's difficult to hit a goat, and it's almost
impossible to avoid hitting a cow.

—P. J. O'Rourke, author

wild card

TELLING DAY FROM NIGHT

During Ramadan, the sacred ninth month of the Muslim year, fasting is practiced daily from sunrise to sunset. In a crowded city where the horizon is rarely visible, it is considered night once you can't tell a black thread from a white one.

—George Sheldon, artist and traveler

fitness and exercise

Dressing Down

When getting ready for a run outside in cooler weather, dress as though it were 20 degrees Fahrenheit warmer than it is.

—Rulesofthumb.org Review Board

house and home

PAINTING A HOUSE

It takes the average person an hour to paint 1,000 square feet, plus an additional hour for each window or door.

—Rebecca Crowell, artist

sports and recreation

Victory in the Palm of Your Hand

When playing a game of Rock, Paper, Scissors, always start with paper. Most people go for rock because it's the shape a hand forms most easily.

—John Tunney, U. K.

science

LUNAR LETTERS

It is easy to tell whether the moon you see tonight will be bigger or smaller tomorrow night. In the Northern Hemisphere, the moon spells DOC each month. First it looks like a *D* (waxing moon and getting bigger each night), then an *O* (full), then a *C* (waning moon and getting smaller each night). South of the equator, it's reversed and spells COD.

—Kate Gladstone

green living

BY THE BUSLOAD

Every full bus keeps 40 cars off the road.

—the New York Metropolitan Transportation Authority

food and drink

CONTEMPLATING A NAVEL

Pick navel oranges with a more distinct "navel" than just a small hole on the end. It indicates a sweeter orange.

—Rulesofthumb.org Review Board

gambling

PLAYING POKER

When it's your turn to call, don't. Instead, raise or fold.

—Dale Armstrong, cardplayer

health and body

SOCIAL DRINKING

To maintain an even keel at an important social event, make every other drink seltzer or water.

—Gordon Graham, writer

wild card

USING THE DRIVE-THRU WINDOW If there are more than three cars in line ahead of you at a drive-thru window, it'll be faster to get out of the car and go inside.

—Bill Lowe

automobiles

Saving Time at a Toll

Avoid any line with a motorcycle. The biker won't have the money ready. Instead, he'll have to dig into his pocket, and on a cold day he'll have to take off his gloves.

—Benjamin Keh

joker

KEG-TO-LOO RATIO

One toilet per keg of beer.

—Rulesofthumb.org Review Board

the arts

LIP REEDING

To find the correct place to put your lips on a clarinet reed, put a small piece of paper into the tapered slot between the reed and the mouthpiece. Where the paper stops is the correct place for your lips.

—Mandy Reinert

writing and presentation

Revising a Novel

When you think you're done revising a novel, set it aside for three months. Then read through it again to see if it's ready to send out.

—David Malki, filmmaker and cartoonist

conversation and body language

MUTUAL MISUNDERSTANDING

In foreign countries, talk to people who speak a second language that you know too. Two people who both know a little of the same language will communicate better than one who is fluent and one who is not.

—Peter Reimuller

health and body

FURIOUS BRUSHING

If you're not going through four toothbrushes a year, you're not brushing your teeth enough.

—Gerald Gutlipp, mathematician

construction and architecture

ROUNDING UP CABINETS

A curved cabinet will take four times the materials used to build a regular one.

—Art Midvale

food and drink

FLOATING YOUR OATS

You have enough milk in the bowl when the edge of your pile of Cheerios first starts to move.

—Mike Rambo

relationships and romance

LOOKING LIKE A HOT PROSPECT

Avoid groups of four or more people of the same sex in bars. Losers generally travel in packs. Winners won't travel in groups of three or more if they're seriously looking for other winners.

—Rulesofthumb.org Review Board

weather and temperature

FEASTING BEFORE A STORM

If you see deer out feeding in the early afternoon, expect a change for the worse in the weather within 24 to 48 hours.

—Glen Fritz

cooking and entertaining

FLIPPING FLAPJACKS

It's time to flip your pancakes when the edges look dry.

—Rulesofthumb.org Review Board

business and sales

The Marketing Rule of Three

Your new product should have at least three easily recognizable advantages over its competition.

—Lloyd Barringer, sales representative

money and finance

KNOWING WHERE TO SPEND MONEY Never go cheap on your bed or your shoes. You will be in one or the other your entire life.

—David Schaner

joker

Using Public Washrooms

In a public washroom, always use the toilet farthest away from the door. It's typically cleaner and used less than the others.

—Tony Campo Jr., sales representative for food service equipment

pets

UNDERSTANDING CAT TAILS

A cat's tail is a "semaphore." If the tail curls in the shape of an *S*, your cat is as happy as a clam. If it's standing straight up, it's saying, "Hi, how are you today?" If the tail is off to one side, your cat wants to play. If it's down to the ground or twitching, it's in a bad mood.

—Tonea Altos

hobbies

COVERING A COUCH

It takes between 10 and 12 yards of fabric to reupholster a full-size sofa.

—Phil Tomlinson, woodworker

animals and wildlife

PRETTY BIRD

The more attractive and colorful the bird, the more likely that it is the male of the species.

—Rulesofthumb.org Review Board

recreational vehicles

DODGING CAR DOORS

Allow a distance of about four feet between your bicycle and parked cars to keep from running into an opening door or a person exiting a car.

—Charles Shapiro

house and home

SOFT WATER GONE HARD

You can tell if your water is hard or soft by looking at your ice cubes. Hard-water cubes have a white spot in the center where minerals congregate; soft-water cubes are uniformly cloudy.

—Lou J. Smith, executive director of Canadian Water Quality Association

safety and survival

FINDING A MISSING PERSON

Missing hikers are usually found within four miles of where they were last seen, the elderly within a mile, and suicides within one-quarter mile.

—Marilyn Greene

style and appearance

A TUX FOR ALL SEASONS

If you need to wear a tuxedo at least once a year, it pays to buy one and avoid the ordeal of renting. They last a long time and rarely go out of style.

—Doug Weaver, accountant

education and school

Hitting the Books

To ace a course, plan on spending two hours on outside study and homework for every hour of classroom time.

—Rulesofthumb.org Review Board

wild card

Express-Line Etiquette

On a "10 items or less" checkout line, multiples of the same product may be fairly counted as a single item.

—Rulesofthumb.org Review Board

food and drink

HIGH AND DRY WINES

The drier the wine, the higher the alcohol level.

—Paul Grim, wine salesman

education and school

MAJORING IN PROCRASTINATION

Chronic high school procrastinators need to double the time required to pull off a last-minute crunch in college. If you typically waited until 6 hours before the due date in high school, you'll need 12 hours at the college level.

—Anne Wachtel

pets

FEEDING THE KITTY Feed your cat twice a day, giving it as much as it will eat in 30 minutes.

—Ronald Newberry

sports and recreation
STRINGING A YO-YO
The string for your yo-yo should reach from the floor to your belly button. However, shorter strings are good for loops and long ones are best for string tricks.

—Bill Alton

money and finance
BUYING UP THE BOONIES
Never offer more than two thirds the asking price for rural land.

—Ren Heim, landscaper

cooking and entertaining
HOLDING THE MAYO (TOGETHER)
When making homemade mayonnaise, add one bottle cap of vinegar or lemon juice for every egg yolk before you start mixing in the oil. This stabilizes the mass and helps to prevent the oil from separating.

—Tim Allen

business and sales

SEALING THE CAR DEAL

Stop selling and close the deal when your customer asks what colors are available.

—Dirck Z. Meengs, management consultant

food and drink

ROUTE SIXTY-SICK

Avoid any restaurants with a name containing the route number where they're located.

—Rulesofthumb.org Review Board

wild card

Swarming Bees

Honeybees will start to congregate in a horseshoe-shaped pattern on the front of the hive three days before they start to swarm.

—Anthony Sykes, orchard worker

food and drink

THE DAILY GRIND

If your coffee is too strong, the grind is too fine. If your coffee is too weak, the grind is too coarse.

—Rulesofthumb.org Review Board

travel

Wagon-Train Rations

For long trips and expeditions, plan on taking at least two pounds of food per person per day.

—G. Brooks

computers and technology

BUYING A STEREO

Your system will sound as good as your speakers. The speakers should cost at least as much as the two next-most-expensive components put together.

—Jeff Brown

recreational vehicles

CALCULATING A BOAT'S FASTEST SPEED The effective maximum speed in knots can be determined by multiplying the square root of the boat's length in feet by 1.3.

—Tim Yen, engineer and naval architect

green living

MADE IN THE SHADE

One large tree has the cooling power of five average air conditioners running 20 hours a day.

—Debra Prybyla, writer for *The New York State Conservationist*

sports and recreation

SWATTING A FLY

Wait for the fly to land on a hard surface and move its front two legs to its face in a feeding or cleaning action, then swat.

—Martin Parker

health and body

GOING VIRAL

If a patient complains about a sore throat or a runny nose or an upset stomach, he or she probably has a bacterial infection. But if the patient complains about a sore throat, a runny nose, *and* an upset stomach, he or she has a viral infection.

—Russell T. Johnson

career and work life

STICKING TO SCHEDULE

The average person can attach 400 to 450 pressure-sensitive address labels to envelopes per hour. An ambitious worker can do 800.

—David Updike, president of the Mail Box of Ithaca

house and home

RINGING UP GROCERIES

Figure $3 per item to estimate the cost of your groceries at the checkout counter. Inflation is not a factor; as prices rise, packages shrink.

—Penny Russell

style and appearance

The Bald Truth

Toupees never look like the real thing. They appear either cheap or like a "good one."

—Rulesofthumb.org Review Board

advertising and design

Home Run Sponsorship

Putting $1,000 behind a sports event will generate about the same exposure as $10,000 in advertising.

—from *The Wall Street Journal*

joker

ARGUING A CASE

If you have the facts, pound the facts; if you have the law, pound the law; if you have neither, pound the table.

—Jeff Eckard, lawyer and entrepreneur

cooking and entertaining

COOKING A STEAK

If you want a medium-rare steak, it should be as firm as the puffy area between your thumb and your index finger. If you want your steak rarer, it should be softer, and if more done, it should be harder.

—J. Harb, sous-chef for Restaurant La Residence

construction and architecture

TIME TO BUILD A HOUSE

It takes four experienced builders about 400 hours to build an average-size house.

—Thomas Peterson, builder

math and measurements

DEVELOPING A TASTE FOR METRIC WEIGHTS

For estimating metric weights:

100 g = a double-decker hamburger

500 g = a lobster

1 kg = a bag of brown sugar

2 kg = a bag of flour

4 kg = an arm-hugging bag of dog food

—Rulesofthumb.org Review Board

safety and survival

SURFING WITH CONFIDENCE

If you see a school of porpoises, the water is free of sharks.

—Joseph Liberkowski, ex–lifeguard

children and child care

MARCHING WITH SMALL-FRY When walking with small children who fall behind, the slower you walk, the slower they will walk. If you maintain your pace, they will keep up with you, albeit somewhat behind.

—Carl Mixon

food and drink

Hold the Crabs

Crabbing season in Texas consists of all the months with the letter *r* in them. You can catch crabs during the other months, but they aren't very good to eat.

—David Hechler

law and crime

RHETORICAL QUESTIONING

When questioned by a police officer, assume that he already knows the answers to most of the questions he's asking you.

—Rulesofthumb.org Review Board

conversation and body language

ADDRESSING CLERGY

Always call a Roman Catholic priest "Father" unless he is wearing some purple. Then address him as "Bishop" or "Your Excellency."

—Rev. Halsey Howe,
Saint Mark's Church

politics

Judging the Polls

Never trust a political poll that is missing a full attribution and a full disclosure of its methodology. Anything less should be considered political spin.

—Luke Losada

writing and presentation

MEASURED SPEECH

To estimate how long a speech will take to deliver in minutes, count the number of words and divide by 150.

—Jeremy Rose, adjunct professor

business and sales

TOUGH LOVE

Managers tend to be attentive to people they like, and to avoid the ones that give them problems. Don't neglect your favorites, but make sure to pay attention to the problems of the troublesome people. To succeed, you have to win over the whole group, not just the ones who cooperate.

—S. L. Young, project manager

sports and recreation

Gigging for Frogs

Never spear a frog whose eyes are wider apart than your fist. Anything wider might not be a frog at all, and it has its eyes on you.

—Rulesofthumb.org Review Board

fitness and exercise

THE RAP ON REPS

When working out with an exercise machine, choose a weight setting that lets you do 8 to 12 repetitions comfortably. If you struggle to get beyond 5, the setting is too heavy. If you complete 10 without feeling any fatigue at all, it is too light.

—Kelly Rogers

cooking and entertaining

WHIPPING UP A STEW

To make a stew without a recipe, use approximately equal amounts of all the main ingredients, and double that amount of starch (rice, potatoes, etc.).

—Gail Smith

career and work life

TERMINATING QUESTIONS To find out why you were fired, check out the requirements/expectations in the job listing for your former position and look for any new additions.

—Michael Stormer, project manager

health and body

AVOIDING MOTION SICKNESS

If you are prone to car or bus travel sickness, try looking out the window, preferably forward, and do not read.

—Eldad Benary

weather and temperature

YOUR LOCAL WEATHER BUG

To get a rough estimate of the temperature outdoors in degrees Fahrenheit, count the number of times a lone cricket chirps in 15 seconds and add 37.

—Steven Harper

safety and survival

ESCAPING A CROCODILE ATTACK

Zigzag to outrun a crocodile.

—Rulesofthumb.org Review Board

business and sales

RUNNING AN AIRLINE

Every penny more per gallon of fuel cost adds $195 million to the airline industry's expenses per year.

—John Heimlich, chief economist for
Air Transport Association of America

food and drink

BOXCAR BERRIES

Blackberries tend to grow where hobos camp or wait for freight trains outside old rail yards.

—Gary Wheeler

style and appearance

WARDROBE WARRIORS

When shopping for clothes, quickly scan the rack or display from a distance. Any items that stand out are probably ones you'd enjoy wearing without second-guessing yourself. If nothing catches your eye, move on.

—Rulesofthumb.org Review Board

the arts
STREAMLINING YOUR BOOK COLLECTION

If you don't remember what a book is about, you don't need it. Donate it to your local library.

—Rulesofthumb.org Review Board

pets
Saddling Up Right

If your stirrup is the right length, you should be able to look over your knee and see the tip of your toe when you sit in the saddle.

—John H. Beauvais

money and finance
TEXT MESSAGE TALLY

A text message of more than six lines will likely be sent *and billed* as two messages.

—Fabian Hemmrt

joker

MAKING A CHIMP GO APE

Never walk past a chimpanzee while wearing a clown suit.

—Todd Strong, circus school student

animals and wildlife

Tails of the Sea

Fish have vertical tails. Sea mammals have horizontal tails.

—Rulesofthumb.org Review Board

recreational vehicles

WHEN NOT TO ROW YOUR BOAT

If there are three or more inches of water in the bilge of a rowboat, don't get in it. Your weight will be enough to capsize it.

—Andrew Kuchinsky

relationships and romance

LOVE STRUCK . . . OR NOT If the object of your affection does not make you a bit nervous, at least in the beginning, it's not love.

—Rulesofthumb.org Review Board

sports and recreation

Making Friends Online

When playing *World of Warcraft*, night elves and warlocks will help you on your quest. Players who are warriors or human paladins will not.

—Rachel, *World of Warcraft* player

the arts

ANIMATING ANIMATION

Animated characters are more lifelike if their actions are slightly sped up.

—Scott Marsh

children and child care

WATER WORKS

If all else fails when trying to pacify a baby, try holding him or her near running water.

—Rulesofthumb.org Review Board

animals and wildlife

KEEPING YOURSELF IN ELEPHANT MEAT

One elephant will provide as much meat as 100 antelopes.

—Pygmy hunters in Zaire, from *NOVA*

---

conversation and body language

GRILLING WITH APLOMB

Save the difficult or unpleasant questions until the end of the interview. But try to finish with something polite, that is if the interviewee is still talking to you.

—Jennifer Evans

education and school

Carefully Worded Essays

Answer an essay question as if you were talking to your parents.

—Dean Sheridan, electronics technician

food and drink

CHURCH BASEMENT COFFEE

A one-pound can of regular grind tossed into a commercial urn will brew 50 cups of decent coffee or 60 cups of weak coffee. A pound and a half of regular grind will make 90 cups of decent coffee.

—John Brink, building superintendent

hobbies

MAKING CLOTHES

Always sew the seams on a garment from the hem up.

—Madeleine Yardley, art teacher

math and measurements

Estimating Crowd Size

To get an accurate estimate of a crowd, add the maximum number reported by the supporters of the event and the minimum reported by detractors and divide by three.

—Anders Sandberg, computational neuroscientist

advertising and design

SIZING UP NAME BADGES If you're designing name badges for a conference or other event, make the guests' names big enough to be read from eight to ten feet away. That way people can read the badges without having to awkwardly lean in and stare at each other's chest. (The event name, location, dates, etc., can be tiny; everyone knows where they are and why.)

—Rulesofthumb.org Review Board

wild card

Avoiding a Flag Faux Pas

The hoist of a flag (its width) should be one fifth the height of the flagpole. So on a 25-foot flag pole, fly a 5' × 8' flag.

—Rulesofthumb.org Review Board

gambling

BLADDER TIP-OFF

Never bet on a dog that urinates just before a race. Either it is nervous and will burn out early, or it is too full of water and will be slow.

—Bob Horton, statistics consultant

business and sales

CUTTING A DEAL

When negotiating for money, pay attention to when your opponent's increments of change begin to decrease in size; that's when he or she is close to a bargaining limit.

—Jeff Furman, business consultant and cofounder of Ben & Jerry's

writing and presentation

TAKE IT FROM THE TOP

When writing a magazine article, begin with a snappy lead sentence, then write the piece to match the tone of the lead. Before submitting the article, delete the lead sentence.

—Gordon Hard, *Consumer Reports*

health and body

LUMP SUM

Estimate the approximate number of calories it takes to maintain your weight by multiplying your current weight by 15. To lose or gain weight, alter your calorie intake by 20 percent in the desired direction.

—F. Jill Charboneau, college instructor and consultant

cooking and entertaining

CHECKING DRIED VEGETABLES

Properly dried peas and corn should shatter when hit with a hammer.

—Betsy Cook

automobiles

THE BEST DAY FOR A GOOD DEAL

Wanting their monthly reports to look good, the sales staff is more likely to bargain on the last day of the month.

—Rulesofthumb.org Review Board

construction and architecture

Building a Dock

Figure $20 a square foot for deck space plus $750 for every piling pounded in by a pile driver when putting in a dock.

—Bill George

business and sales

CHATTING AT A TRADE SHOW

When working a booth, you should chat briefly with at least 100 people per day. Ten percent of those people are likely to be good leads.

—Allen Konopacki

travel

Mini Mouth's Menus

If expenses are a consideration when visiting Disney World, order children's meals for everybody. The portions are adequate, and the prices are reasonable.

—John Thedford

safety and survival

BARKING A COMMANDING ORDER

If you are on the scene of an emergency and need help, point to one specific person and say "You, call 911." This gets the individual involved in a personal way whereas saying "Someone call 911" will not.

—Rulesofthumb.org Review Board

computers and technology

AMASSING MUSIC

An iPod can hold 1,000 to 1,250 songs per five gigs of storage.

—Joe Cleary

food and drink

BREWING A PERFECT POT Use one heaping teaspoon of tea per drinker, then add one more "for the pot."

—Rulesofthumb.org Review Board

health and body

A HEADSET THAT GOES TO ELEVEN

If you have to remove your headphones to hear people talking to you, the volume is too loud.

—Jane Spencer

automobiles

OUTSMARTING PARKING GARAGE SIGNS

Even if the garage has a flashing "full" sign, it isn't full unless the entrance is physically blocked.

—Owen T. Anderson

green living

UTILITIES NOT INCLUDED

You can expect a 40 percent reduction in energy consumption when a tenant assumes responsibility for the energy bills.

—Larry Beck

law and crime

SIMPLY PUT

The more succinct a lawyer's argument, the more confident he or she is of victory.

—Rulesofthumb.org Review Board

wild card

Blasting a Stump

You can blow most tree stumps out of the ground if you use one stick of dynamite for every four inches of stump diameter. (Trees with taproots take less.)

—Joe Kaiser

safety and survival

SNUFFING OUT A FIRE

Direct your fire extinguisher at the base of the flames from a distance of less than ten feet. If you can't get any closer than ten feet, the fire is probably too large for a handheld fire extinguisher.

—Norman Lewis, volunteer fireman

joker

Roadside Trash

Two out of every three magazines tossed along the roadsides will be pornographic.

—Rusty Cartmill

advertising and design

PHOTO MOJO

In advertising, art, and photography, the direction the subject is looking and the flow of the composition affect the tone of an image. Left is the past, right is the future, up is positive, down is negative. So a subject looking up and to the right is looking positively into the future.

—Jeremy Reid, graphic designer

science

SCIENCE FAIR TRAINING

You need a minimum of five trials on a science fair experiment if you want to have meaningful results.

—Shawn Carlson, Ph.D., science educator

business and sales

BUYING FILING CABINETS To estimate the number of filing cabinets you need, consider that the average document is 2.5 pages and the average drawer holds 2,500 pages. That means you need one drawer for every 1,000 documents.

—Rulesofthumb.org Review Board

pets

THIS OLD KENNEL

A kennel should be two times the length of the dog you are building it for. Measure the dog from its nose to the tip of its tail.

—Charles Stoehr

sports and recreation

FISHING OUT OF YOUR DEPTH

When in doubt, fish a lake deep to shallow rather than shallow to deep.

—Rulesofthumb.org Review Board

money and finance

POP'S PIGGY BANK

Every dollar you save in your twenties supplies one dollar of monthly retirement income in your sixties.

—Elaine Lyon, tax adviser

cooking and entertaining

GOOD GRAVY

For thickening soups and sauces, you can use cornstarch instead of flour. The equivalency is one tablespoon of cornstarch equals two tablespoons of flour.

—Kay Parker

health and body

The Thumb-Value Rule

A thumb is worth 40 percent of the whole hand in worker's compensation cases.

—Rulesofthumb.org Review Board

food and drink

SPOTTING A HOT CHILE PEPPER

The darker the color, the more pointed the tip, and the narrower the shoulders, the hotter the pepper will be.

—Jane Butel, author of *Chili Madness*

fitness and exercise

Forecasting Your Finish

You can predict your marathon time by multiplying your best ten-kilometer time by 4.65.

—Jack Daniels, physiologist

sports and recreation

FIRST-ROUND HOCKEY PICKS

When playing a pickup game of hockey, look for the guy with old, beat-up equipment. He's probably really good, and you should try to be on his team.

—Frank Cleary, teacher and physicist

career and work life

LANDING A POSITION

When looking for a new job, expect one to five job leads and/or interviews for every 100 résumés you mail out.

—Karen O'Neill, career consultant

conversation and body language

GREAT MINDS LAUGH ALIKE

At a party or public event, any person who laughs spontaneously at the same time you do is worth cultivating as a friend.

—Kelly Yeaton, teacher and stage manager

safety and survival

NATURAL COMPASS

The tips of tall, pointed trees such as spruce usually lean slightly to the north of east.

—Alwyn T. Perrin, editor of *Explorers Ltd. Source Book*

food and drink

FRESH SOUNDS

Listening to the sounds certain fruits and vegetables make will often clue you in to how fresh they are. For example, a fresh artichoke squeaks when you squeeze its leaves, a ripe watermelon makes a "punk" sound instead of a "pank" or "pink" when you tap it, and a ripe pineapple has a sound similar to one made when you tap the inside of your wrist.

—Rulesofthumb.org Review Board

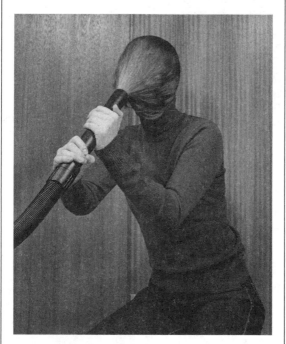

computers and technology

BREAKING IN A NEW GADGET After buying new electronic equipment, use it for 48 hours straight. If it doesn't fail, it probably won't.

—Rulesofthumb.org Review Board

hobbies

IMPROVING TOMATO TASTE

When planting tomato seedlings, crush some eggshells (one to two eggs' worth) and put them in the hole with the seedling. The shells will promote the growth of large and more flavorful tomatoes.

—Rulesofthumb.org Review Board

weather and temperature

Web Sites for Weather

If there's dew on the spiderwebs in the grass in the morning, it won't rain.

—Pete Stewart

the arts

PLANTING EVIDENCE

If there is a pistol on the wall in the first act, it should be fired by the third act.

—Bob Larson, quoting Anton Chekhov

health and body

Height Expectations

To predict children's final adult height, double their height on their second birthday.

—Edward Blackman, physician

automobiles

SMOKE SIGNALS

Blue smoke from the exhaust means the car may need a complete engine overhaul. Black smoke usually indicates a maladjusted carburetor. White smoke could mean a leaking head gasket if the engine has been warmed (ignore it if the engine is cold).

—Norman Evans

business and sales

BAD CUSTOMERS RISING

Customers are most difficult to deal with during the full moon. The next most trying phase is the new moon.

—Georgia Chapman, pharmacist

sports and recreation

A SAND CASTLE FIT FOR A KING

To build a sturdy sand castle, the sand should be firm enough that your footprints barely show.

—Rulesofthumb.org Review Board

wild card

POSTING A LETTER

You can mail five sheets of paper with one first-class stamp.

—Ron Bean

animals and wildlife

DETERMINING AN ALLIGATOR'S LENGTH

The distance between an alligator's eyes in inches is equal to its length in feet.

—Joan Isbell

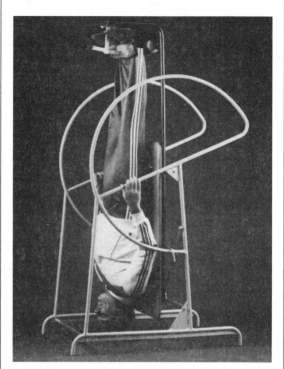

fitness and exercise

THE REST OF A DAY Allow 24 hours of recovery for every hour of highly stressful workout.

—Ned Frederick, writer

safety and survival

PROTECTING YOUR EARS

An earplug is properly sized if two thirds of it fits inside the ear canal and one third remains exposed.

—Rulesofthumb.org Review Board

recreational vehicles

Flying by a Thunderstorm

If you're flying toward a stationary thunderstorm in the Northern Hemisphere, try to pass it on the right. You'll get a tailwind.

—Neil Klohmann, airline pilot

writing and presentation

GETTING TO THE POINT

When editing an article, you rarely go wrong crossing out the first page and a half.

—Bryant Robey, founding editor of *American Demographics*

house and home

DIY Plumbing Excursions

No matter how simple, it seems that all do-it-yourself plumbing projects require three trips to the hardware store.

—Robin Wilkinson

politics

COUNTING ON VOTERS

Target 65 percent of your total campaign expenditures for voter contact—if you are spending more than 35 percent on non-voter contact, adjust your priorities.

—Jim Arnold

money and finance

LOOKING A GIFT HORSE ...

The value of the gifts you receive at a wedding will be no more than one third the cost of staging the event.

—Warren Harris

green living

FERTILE MEASURES

When spreading manure, figure one handful of poultry manure is equal to a shovelful of cow manure because the former is much higher in nitrogen.

—Rulesofthumb.org Review Board

cooking and entertaining

MAKING TOFU

One pound of soybeans yields two and a half pounds of tofu.

—Rob Shapiro

health and body

LOOKING OUT FOR YOUR DOMINANT EYE

To find your dominant eye, make a circle of your thumb and forefinger about six inches in front of your face. Look through the circle with both eyes at an object across the room. Now close one eye; if the object stays in the circle, the open eye is the dominant one.

—Donald H. Dunn

food and drink

WELL-STOCKED

If you can get three cases ahead of your consumption, you can stop worrying about having a good supply.

—David Nowicki, wine authority

pets

DOUBLE THE CUTENESS

Never adopt just one kitten. Adopting two is a lot easier for you and better for the kittens because they will entertain each other.

—Andrew Mullen

travel

Trip Tips

Leave the maid about a dollar a night. Leave more at an expensive hotel or if you received any extra service. Leave lots more if you made a mess.

—Rulesofthumb.org Review Board

relationships and romance

CHOOSING A SPOUSE When women marry, they think their husbands will change. When men marry, they think their wives will never change. Both are wrong.

—Bruno Colapietro, matrimonial lawyer

conversation and body language

Calling In an Order

When buying something over the phone, ask for the salesperson's full name. Then he or she is less likely to make a mistake with your order.

—Jennifer Evans

the arts

TUNING WITH A TWIST

A stringed instrument is less apt to slip out of pitch if the strings are tuned up from flat than down from sharp.

—Robbie Aceto, musician

math and measurements

FINGER METRICS

A centimeter is about as long as the width of an adult's pinkie nail.

—Roger Sorbo, science teacher

hobbies

DISHING OUT CLAY

When making a ceramic serving dish, casserole, or bean pot, use one pound of clay for each person you want it to serve. For example, five pounds of clay will make a dish that will serve five people (with second helpings for some).

—Jim Dunn, potter

joker

QUACK REMEDIES

If there are dozens of different remedies for a complaint, you can be sure none of them works.

—Ken Follett, author

education and school

BEFRIENDING THOSE IN THE KNOW

When first teaching at a new school, always make friends with the head-office secretaries. They really run the place and can help far more than the principal.

—Rulesofthumb.org Review Board

house and home

RESCUED IN A FLASH

The fastest way to find a small object on the floor is to look for its shadow, not the object itself. Roll a flashlight around on the floor and the object's shadow will be easy to spot.

—Maitlen W. Montmarency, painter

health and body

GETTING A GRIP ON YOUR BRAIN

Determine the size of your brain by putting your fists together so your wrists touch and your thumbnails face you side by side.

—Rulesofthumb.org Review Board

construction and architecture

Renovating a Commercial Building

Renovation generally saves only 10 to 15 percent of the cost of new construction.

—James Colby, civil engineer

law and crime

Submitting to a Lie Detector Test

If you are innocent, do not take a lie detector test. If you're guilty, take it, because it may exonerate you.

—Kevin Kelly, writer and technologist

joker

GROSS ANATOMY

Human blood volume is equal to about a caseful of beer.

—Kevin Williams

advertising and design

WINNING CONTESTANTS

People will enter a contest based on two factors: ease of entry and incentive to win.

—Charlie Kondek, public relations

sports and recreation

OUT IN LEFT FIELD If you are playing left field and don't know where to throw the ball, toss it to the shortstop.

—Rulesofthumb.org Review Board

safety and survival

SWINGING AN AX . . . SAFELY

The chopping area for using an ax safely should have a radius of the user's outstretched arm plus at least three ax lengths.

—from The Boy Scout Association, *Use of Axes and Saws*

animals and wildlife

TROUGH COUTURE

It takes two pigs to make a pair of pigskin pants.

—Mary Ellen Parker

wild card

DASHING OFF ERRANDS

It will take 20 to 30 minutes to shop for one item if you know exactly what you want and where to go. Thus, if you go out at lunch to buy three different things, plan on being gone for 1 to 1½ hours.

—Jim Kauffold

weather and temperature

IN THE STRIKE ZONE

You can tell how many miles you are from a thunderstorm by counting the seconds between the lightning and thunder and dividing by five.

—Millie Stordeur

cooking and entertaining

STIRRING UP A COCKTAIL PARTY

Make sure to have at least 12 guests at a cocktail party. With fewer guests, the party becomes one conversation in which only one person speaks at a time. But with 12 people, the conversation splits into two or more groups with more chance for interplay and movement.

—Tom Nelson, photographer

house and home

Generating Enough Juice

An electric generator must produce two and a half times the power consumption of the appliance for which you are using it.

—Rulesofthumb.org Review Board

joker

Wearing Out Markers

Buy two black markers for every other color you buy. It is always the first color to go in a set (the green and red go next).

—Carolyn Lloyd

writing and presentation

THE EFFORT IN EFFORTLESS

Effortless prose generally takes three to four drafts.

—Dr. Paul Trotman

gambling

STAKING OUT A TABLE

Choose a poker table that has one or two players who are significantly worse than you. Playing with more than two worse players will not be enjoyable.

—Rulesofthumb.org Review Board

animals and wildlife

THE UDDER END The average milk-producing life of a dairy cow is five to seven years.

—Chris Dahl, dairy farmer

sports and recreation

THE SAILBOARD FOR YOU

To pick out the right size sailboard (sized by liters in volume), add 20 to 40 to your weight. A 150-pound person should sail a board that is 170 to 190 liters in volume for proper buoyancy.

—Jeremy Bishop, windsurfing expert

science

Wiggle Room

Consider plus or minus 3 percent a reasonable error for most lab experiments. More than that and you'd better be prepared to explain it.

—Dr. Gertrude Ward

food and drink

DINING ABROAD

When traveling in a foreign country, avoid restaurants with menus printed in more than two languages; they are for tourists.

—Rulesofthumb.org Review Board

fitness and exercise

THE WALK-AND-TALK WORKOUT

If you can't maintain a comfortable conversation while exercising, you are working beyond your aerobic capacity.

—Kurt Ulrich, exercise specialist

career and work life

CALCULATING YOUR WORTH

When negotiating salary with a recruiter, make your opening figure at least 30 percent more than your present package (including bonus, perks, and next raise). If the new job will involve moving, add another 10 percent.

—Charles Fleming, author of *Executive Pursuit*

the arts

Excessive Shooting

Documentary film makers should plan on shooting ten times the footage that will end up in the finished film.

—Sandra A. Kraft, writer

hobbies

BALANCING SHRUBBERY

Never plant three of the same shrub in a row. Always offset. That way, if one dies, it will be harder to notice.

—Rulesofthumb.org Review Board

food and drink

TIMING A TOLL HOUSE

Chocolate chip cookies are best four minutes after they come out of the oven.

—Marc Pelath

conversation and body language

GENERALLY SPEAKING . . .

People who say "in terms of" usually don't know what they're talking about.

—Elizabeth Kasehagen, R.N., delivery room nurse

sports and recreation

DOING A DAVY CROCKETT

When stalking deer, patience and an extremely slow pace are essential. If you travel more than a quarter of a mile in an hour (that's about four football fields), you're moving too fast.

—J. P. Thomas, deer stalker

health and body

BENDING YOUR GENDER

If you're a man changing your sex, expect to appear 5 years older, because men's faces look more rugged than women's. However, if you're a woman, expect to look 10 to 12 years younger after a sex change. For example, a 30-year-old woman will look and sound like a boy of 18 or 20.

—Marge Willes, counselor for Gateway Gender Alliance

money and finance

FEELING CHARITABLE

You are wealthy enough to give some money to worthy causes when you can buy all the groceries you need.

—Sharon K. Yntema, writer

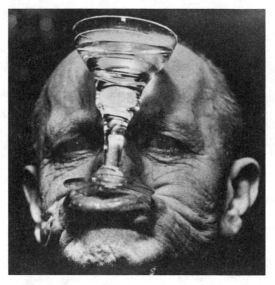

cooking and entertaining

D-RATIONS When you are planning drinks for a party, figure two drinks per guest for the first half hour and one drink per hour after that.

—Lisa Dahl, conference manager

automobiles

THE BOUNCE TEST

To check the condition of your shock absorbers, bounce the car up and down with your foot. If the car keeps on bouncing after you stop, you need new shocks.

—Tom Robinson

sports and recreation

Seeing Through a Glass Darkly

For high-altitude skiing, you need dark sunglasses. Test your glasses by putting them on and looking in a mirror. If you can see your eyes, the glasses aren't dark enough.

—Rulesofthumb.org Review Board

construction and architecture

Stone Walling

Plan on ordering (or collecting) two cubic yards of stone for every cubic yard of finished wall.

—David Finn

business and sales

Door-to-Door Demeanor

After knocking, stand at least four feet back from the door so you're not right in your customer's face when he or she answers.

—Benjamin Snyder, Bible salesman

wild card

Pest Patrol

It takes 16 praying mantis egg cases per acre to keep harmful crop-damaging insects, like grasshoppers and aphids, under control.

—Ronald Newberry

conversation and body language

NEW WORD ON THE STREET

When you hear a new word, you'll hear it again within 24 hours.

—Glenda Oglesby, hypnotherapist

style and appearance

IF THE SOCK FITS . . .

Wrap the bottom part of a sock around your fist. If the sock is the right size, the heel will just meet the toe.

—Nelson Smith, physical education teacher

house and home

DOWNLOADING

When you're moving to a new house, the possessions you get rid of should be equal to at least one third of the possessions you keep.

—Rulesofthumb.org Review Board

children and child care

HYDRATING TODDLERS

Sunken eyeballs in a sick infant indicate at least 10 percent dehydration.

—Dr. James Macmillan

health and body

RECOVERING FROM LSD It takes ten years
to recover from serious use of LSD.

—Leonard Cohen, poet and songwriter

weather and temperature

FOLLOWING FALL

On the East Coast of the United States, the fall foliage change moves south at a rate of 50 miles a day.

—Margaret Wagner

cooking and entertaining

COVER CROPS

Cook vegetables the way they grow: Cook roots, covered, starting them in cold water. Cook greens uncovered in boiling water.

—Kelly Yeaton, quoting *The Mystery Chef,* a 1930s radio cooking guide

business and sales

Hocking Your Stuff

You'll get half the amount a pawnshop thinks the item will bring in if you forfeit it.

—Rulesofthumb.org Review Board

education and school

Lab Tested

If a professor describes a science experiment in class, it will be on the exam.

—Rulesofthumb.org Review Board

sports and recreation

FIRING A FOOTBALL

A quarterback has three seconds to throw the ball; after that he'll get sacked.

—Bob O'Halloran, talk show host for WHBY Radio

politics

WINNING WITH LAST-MINUTE PUSHES

Target roughly 10 percent of the voters needed to win. If you are running a state legislative race and need 15,000 votes to win, you must have at least 1,500 identified supporters whom you will push to the polls by last-minute calls, free car rides, taxis, etc.

—Cathy Allen, political consultant

travel

COMMUTING IN TOKYO

In Tokyo, a bicycle is faster than a car for most trips of less than 50 minutes. A motorcycle, ridden carefully but without regard for the law, is twice as fast as a car.

—David A. Lloyd-James

joker

CORRALLING A BOOR

Do not invite a habitual raconteur to a party if the space is less than 600 square feet, not counting the piano. Otherwise, it will be hard for people to escape him or her without leaving the party.

—John Boyd

cooking and entertaining

CRACKING WITH FINESSE

Always crack an egg on a flat surface. The shell will shatter less, and little shards of it won't wind up in your recipe.

—Jeffrey Buben, chef

money and finance

BUYING AN EYESORE

The best way to make money in residential real estate is to buy the worst home on the best street.

—Rulesofthumb.org Review Board

computers and technology

Managing Hard Drive Space

For a Windows-based computer to run properly you need to have at least twice as much hard drive space available as the amount of RAM. This means a PC with two gigabytes of RAM should have at least four gigabytes of free hard drive space.

—Greg Marshall

food and drink

THE FRESH EGG TEST

When placed in a bowl of water, a fresh egg will sink and lie on its side. An egg that isn't fresh, but still edible, will sink and stand partially erect on its tapered end. A rotten egg will float.

—David Hechler

business and sales

PASSING OUT WORK Don't give an
employee a project after 4:30 unless it can
be completed by 5:00.

—Cally Arthur, editor and communications coordinator

pets

Guessing an Old Gray Mare's Age

A horse develops folds in its eyelids at the age of seven, and one fold is added each year after that.

—Paul Glover

math and measurements

FEELING THE HEAT

One BTU is equal to one wooden kitchen match. One box of wooden kitchen matches contains enough energy to heat up one eight-cup coffeepot.

—Art Loomis, high school teacher

sports and recreation

DRUNKEN DIVERS

The deeper a scuba diver descends, the more nitrogen he absorbs from the air he is breathing, causing an intoxicating condition known as nitrogen narcosis or "rapture of the deep." As a rough measure, every 50 feet of depth is equal to one martini.

—W. Suter

green living

TRASH TALK

The average person generates one ton of garbage per year.

—Ellen Marsh, Library Communications Director of
Cornell University

house and home

TESTING FREEZER TEMPERATURE

A spoon will ring when rapped on a carton of ice cream if your freezer temperature is zero degrees Fahrenheit or colder.

—Rulesofthumb.org Review Board

hobbies

GLAZING A POT

Hold a pot in the glaze for the time it takes your heart to beat four times.

—Kathy Edmondson

the arts

SHOOTING A SCENE

Count at least ten seconds after you press a movie camera's record button before you allow the action to commence. You'll need this buffer zone when editing the footage.

—Flip Schulke, underwater photographer

automobiles

Washing Regularly

Always clean your car before taking it in for service. Mechanics are more likely to take advantage of you if your car looks like it needs "everything."

—Rulesofthumb.org Review Board

safety and survival

CHILLY BIKE RIDES

Wear goggles when you are riding a bike in temperatures below 40 degrees Fahrenheit.

—Tanya Kucak

house and home

ATTEMPTING ELECTRONIC REPAIR If you can't find the last screw when taking apart an electronic device, check under the warranty sticker.

—Joe Cleary

education and school

Keeping Up with Medicine

The half-life of knowledge in medical school is four years. Fifty percent of what you learn as a freshman is obsolete when you graduate.

—Dr. Lawrence Senterfit, microbiologist

health and body

MENSTRUAL MEASURES

A girl will have reached her full height 18 months after she starts to menstruate.

—Hilary Peterson, homemaker

food and drink

HANDY CALORIE COUNTER

To estimate the calories in a wedge of rich dessert, make a fist and place it next to the base of the wedge. Count each knuckle that spans the wedge; each represents approximately 100 calories.

—Ronald Arturi

sports and recreation
WINNING AT CHESS
The sacrifice of one pawn is worth three free moves.

—Rulesofthumb.org Review Board

law and crime
Copping a Plea
If you get arrested for a crime you committed and it's your first offense, skip the lawyer, plead guilty, and take your fine and/or probation. It will save you time and money, and is on par with any deal an attorney can arrange.

—Carl Reddick, probation officer

business and sales
HOW MAY I HELP YOU BUY THIS?
When greeting a customer, make sure your first remark refers directly to the product you hope to sell.

—Mike Hart, appliance dealer

wild card

UP IN THE AIR

When trying to pick between two choices, toss a coin in the air. As soon as it is airborne you will realize what side you are hoping it comes down on.

—Rulesofthumb.org Review Board

construction and architecture

Crew Accruals

Two construction workers can do three times as much work as one, and three workers can do four times as much. However, four workers can do only four times as much work as one.

—Rick Lazarus, residential contractor

sports and recreation

SELECTING A SKI POLE

Pick the right ski pole by turning it upside down and grasping the shaft directly below the basket. If your elbow makes a right angle, the pole is a good length.

—Neil Hess, ski instructor

style and appearance

Wigging Out

A long face needs a full wig, and a round face needs height at the crown. However, a woman with an oval face can wear anything.

—Eva Gabor

recreational vehicles

KIDS IN TOW

When bike riding with your children in a trailer, a trip will take 30 to 40 percent longer than it would if you biked it alone, and possibly longer if you stop often to look at horses. The safe top speed with a trailer is 15 miles per hour.

—Rulesofthumb.org Review Board

joker

USING A RULE OF THUMB

Every rule has at least one exception, except this rule.

—Stephen Verbit, attorney

law and crime

CRACKING A CASE To solve a crime, remember two things: The most obvious solution is probably the correct one; and if you've eliminated all the other possibilities, whatever is left, however improbable, is what happened.

—Howard D. Teten, FBI agent, quoting Sherlock Holmes

food and drink

COFFEE COLORS

If the cream swirls up brown, you have a cup of freshly brewed coffee. If it swirls up gray, the coffee has been sitting on the burner too long.

—Rulesofthumb.org Review Board

sports and recreation

FISH SCALES

A 20-inch brown trout weighs three pounds and a 25-inch one weighs five pounds. For every inch over 25, add one pound to the weight of the fish. So a 27-inch brown trout will weigh approximately seven pounds.

—Thomas Lack

safety and survival

SPOTTING POISON IVY

Leaflets three, let it be.

—Stephen Unsino, poet

green living

Aiming at the Sun

For year-round use, the slope of home hot-water solar collectors should be equal to the latitude at which they are installed.

—Stephen Gibian, architect and stonemason

joker

SHE BITES

As a matter of biology rather than sexism, if an animal or insect bites you, it is probably female.

—Scott M. Kruse, biogeographer

money and finance

A HIGHER DEGREE OF DEBT

Your total debt for student loans should not exceed what you expect to make your first year out of school.

—Rulesofthumb.org Review Board

writing and presentation

BEING HEARD IN A LOUD ROOM

People will quiet down if you speak softly in a noisy room. Speaking louder only encourages more noise.

—Rulesofthumb.org Review Board

house and home

AVOIDING PLUMBING WOES

If you turn off your tap too hard, it will damage the rubber washer, which can be replaced easily. If you let the tap drip, it will erode the metal valve seat, which means a new tap *and* a plumber to install it.

—Dr. Bill Grierson, professor emeritus at the University of Florida

business and sales

SELLING BOOKS

Ten percent of bookstore customers buy 90 percent of the books. Ten percent never buy anything.

—Dave Ewan

pets

THE HOUND NEXT DOOR If you want to be friends with somebody else's dog, let it make the first move, and don't be too quick to respond.

—Walter Pitkin, literary agent

children and child care

GIRLS IN THE MEN'S ROOM

If your daughter is tall enough to stand up and look into the urinal, then she's too old to bring into the men's room.

—Jim Barber, historian

safety and survival

DESCENT NIGHT'S SLEEP

To avoid altitude sickness, don't sleep more than 1,000 feet higher than you did the night before. You can ascend higher during the day to establish routes, but you should descend to the 1,000-foot interval before settling down for the night.

—Dr. David Kumaki

health and body

EATING OILY FISH

The oilier the fish, the higher it is in heart-healthy omega-3 fatty acids.

—Karl Grummich, pharmacist

career and work life

THE LUMBERYARD LOADING RULE

If there is an odd number of items, let the customer load the first one. If there is an even number of items, let the customer load the first two.

—Rulesofthumb.org Review Board

gambling

Choosing Your Game

Never bet when the house advantage is more than 1.5 percent. In U.S. casinos, this means you can play blackjack, baccarat, and craps, but nothing else.

—Marvin Karlins, Ph.D.,
author of *Psyching Out Vegas*

automobiles

SHOPPING FOR FUEL

If you need gas while driving on an interstate, look for exits with at least two gas stations. The competition will mean a lower price per gallon.

—Bob Horton,
statistics
consultant

recreational vehicles

Making Time in a Kayak

In moderate white water, expect to average about four to five miles per hour if you paddle straight downriver and don't stop to play.

—Martha Betcher

cooking and entertaining

THIN-SKINNED LOBSTERS

Lobsters are very susceptible to chemicals and aerosol sprays used in the vicinity of tanks. As a rule, anything that will kill a fly will kill a lobster more quickly.

—T. M. Prudden, lobster expert

wild card

FINDING A FREE RIDE

The potential value of a fare card on the ground is in inverse proportion to the distance it is from the closest transportation stop.

—Lawrence Quigley

the arts

MONSTER ENTERS LEFT

Horror film makers know that the human eye has a tendency to drift slightly to the right side of the screen when viewing a movie, so they have the shocks and surprises come from the left side.

—Will Musham, composer and writer

travel

CRIMSON CAVERNS

In the colder parts of a country, you will often find caves in areas where the soil is red.

—David McClurg, speleologist

pets

HEATING AN AQUARIUM

To determine the wattage for an aquarium heater, allow three watts per gallon in a room of normal temperature. Use four watts per gallon for rooms that are cooler than normal.

—Rulesofthumb.org Review Board

conversation and body language

EXITING AN AWKWARD ENCOUNTER If you meet someone in a public place and are forced to stop and chat against your will, make a polite exit at the first pause that is greater (in seconds) than the number of years since you last spoke.

—James Erwin

house and home

SEEING THE BIG PICTURE

The ideal viewing distance is two and a half times the diagonal width of your television screen.

—Rulesofthumb.org Review Board

sports and recreation

Throwing a Punch

You've delivered an effective blow if your opponent lifts one foot clear off the ground.

—Angelo Dundee, boxing authority

relationships and romance

THE TRAVEL PARTNER RULE

Never plan a vacation with a new partner that is farther into the future than the time you've been together. For example, if you've been dating for only two months, don't plan a vacation three months in the future.

—Jim Veihdeffer, PR pundit

weather and temperature

Earthshaking Prediction

The likelihood of an earthquake goes up if a period of heavy rain lasting a week or more is closely followed by a new or full moon.

—Elaine Gibbons

cooking and entertaining

PREPPIN' FOR A PICNIC

When making potato salad, figure on one and a half medium potatoes and one egg per person.

—Rulesofthumb.org Review Board

business and sales

NAMING A NEW PRODUCT

Americans will not buy something they cannot pronounce.

—Robert M. McMath, new products guru

construction and architecture

BEDRIDDEN

A hospital should have four beds for every thousand people in the community it serves.

—Doug Pineo

food and drink

WORD OF MOUTH GONE SOUTH

If a customer likes your restaurant, he'll tell two other people. If a customer hates your restaurant, he'll tell seven other people.

—Jeff Hamilton, ex-waiter

computers and technology

Seeing the Little Picture

You can make a digital GIF image smaller without sacrificing quality by converting it to a high-quality JPEG file. But it's not worth messing with a GIF image that is smaller than 100 kilobytes.

—Mike White, independent IT consultant

health and body

BREAKING UP WITH YOUR THERAPIST

It is time to stop therapy when you forget your appointment and don't feel bad about it.

—Franklin Crawford, writer

conversation and body language

KEEPING PEOPLE AT BAY

Crossing your arms will make you less apt to be approached.

—Evan Christensen, unemployed

the arts

Giving Up on a Movie

If you get the urge to walk out on a movie after 10 minutes, stick with it; you may change your mind. If you still have the urge after 45 minutes, it's probably not going to get better.

—Rulesofthumb.org Review Board

travel

RE-ORIENT EXPRESS Culture shock occurs only in the first three foreign countries you visit; after that you'll subconsciously focus on similarities rather than differences.

—Gary Gaile, geographer

science

Budgeting Physics Experiments

The shorter the life of the particle, the more it costs to make.

—Scott Parker, data specialist

money and finance

BARON NECESSITIES

In order to make a profit on a piece of land, a developer must construct a building worth at least four times what the land is worth.

—Rulesofthumb.org Review Board

hobbies

SHEEP TO SHAWL

Plan on making one sweater for every two pounds of wool you shear from a sheep.

—Mary Catherine

advertising and design
WORD CONSERVATION

When writing an ad, use sentences composed of 12 words or less.

—David Ogilvy, cofounder of
The Ogilvy and Mather Agency

house and home
That Sinking Feeling

If your swimming pool loses a quarter inch or more of water in a 24-hour period, it's a leak, not evaporation.

—Don Mattox

sports and recreation
GOLFING INTO THE WIND

On a windy day, club down for every 10 mph of wind. If you would normally hit a seven iron approach to a specific green, then use a six iron when the wind is blowing at 10 mph. And with a 20 mph wind, use a five iron on that same shot.

—Jim Johnston, PGA professional

safety and survival

LOST PRIORITIES

When lost, look for shelter, then water. Most people worry about food but are typically found before starvation is ever a real concern.

—Kevin Williams

politics

ANTICIPATING VOTER TURNOUT

The percentage of voter turnout is approximately equal to the age of the voters.

You can expect:

20 percent of 20-year-olds,
30 percent of 30-year-olds,
40 percent of 40-year-olds,
50 percent of 50-year-olds, and
60 percent of 60-year-olds.

—from the Voter Education Task Force

style and appearance

THE RIGHT SHADE OF TONGUE

For TV appearances, match the color of your makeup to the color of the tip of your tongue.

—Sharon K. Yntema, writer

law and crime

Proving Yourself in Court

When testifying before a jury, remember that the other side's attorney wants to make you look flustered. Always sound calm and sure of yourself, regardless of how fast your heart is pounding.

—Rulesofthumb.org Review Board

automobiles

THE COLOR OF RESALE VALUE

When buying a new car, choose a color that matches the ads for your particular model. That's the color most likely to grab a used-car buyer's eye.

—Rich and Jean Taylor Constantine

writing and presentation

LEADING A SEMINAR

If you are leading a seminar, allow six seconds for a response to your call for questions. If someone is going to ask one, he or she will do so within six seconds. After that, keep it moving.

—Tom Werner, management consultant

house and home

APPRECIATING BUSHES It takes ten years
for newly planted trees or shrubs to add
value to your property.

—James Erwin

joker

PICKING ON PUBLIC TRANSPORTATION

The more websites devoted to complaining about the public transit system in a city, the better the system is.

—Don Marti, editor

style and appearance

Brushing Your Hair

Twenty-five brushstrokes per day is considered optimal for distributing natural oils. More brushing causes damage.

—Dr. Jonathan Zizmor, hair and skin expert

fitness and exercise

SWEATING AWAY THE HOURS

After one month of regular exercise, you need one to three hours less sleep each night. This means that working out costs you no waking hours after the first month.

—Rulesofthumb.org Review Board

food and drink

CORKING AN APPETITE

Wine before meals increases hunger. Wine during a meal quells the appetite. Wine at the end of a meal can drown the desire for dessert.

—Maria Simonson

construction and architecture

FRONT ROW PARKING

Include at least one handicapped spot for every 50 parking spaces. In some places, especially southern states, more may be required.

—Rulesofthumb.org Review Board

wild card

JUDGING FIREWORKS

If you see blue fireworks, you are watching a top-notch display.

—Dr. John A. Conkling, executive director of American Pyrotechnics Association

conversation and body language

Spotting a Drunk

If someone wipes his mouth right after taking a drink, he has probably been overindulging.

—Rulesofthumb.org Review Board

health and body

POPPING M&M'S

Fifty-four M&M's have the same caffeine content as two cups of coffee.

—Lynne Boysen

education and school

TRICK QUESTION

Some answers in a multiple-choice test will try to take advantage of a common misconception. If you recognize the misconception, you've eliminated one of the possible answers.

—Felix Mitchell

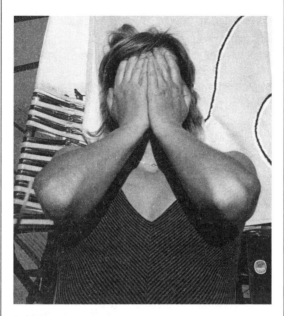

hobbies

"CATCHING" YOUR SUBJECT The more comfortable you make your subject, the better the portrait will be.

—Greg Henshall, industrial photographer

green living

Moving Cargo

One gallon of gas can move a ton of goods 200 miles by rail and 500 miles by inland barge but only 50 miles by large truck. The food on the average American table gets trucked 1,500 miles before being consumed, so buying local saves lots of fuel.

—Luke Losada

animals and wildlife

ELEPHANT EARS

The African elephant has ears shaped like Africa. The Indian elephant has ears shaped like India.

—Norman Brenner

cooking and entertaining

ICING ON THE CAKE

If frosting a round, two-layer cake, use one third of the frosting between the two layers, a third on the top surface, and a third for the side of the cake.

—Rulesofthumb.org Review Board

safety and survival

THE CUTOFF POINT

You can safely cut back in front of the car you are passing when you see its headlights in your inside rearview mirror.

—Leslie Simpson

children and child care

READING FOR BEGINNERS

To teach children how to find books at their own reading level, tell them to open a book near the middle and read from the top of any full page. If there are five words they don't know before getting to the end of the page, the book is too hard for them.

—Eliza Brownrigg Graue, author of
Is Your Child Gifted?

sports and recreation

PICKING A TENT

Figure on 18 square feet of surface area for each adult camper.

—Alan R. Reno

business and sales

RUNNING A VOLUNTEER ORGANIZATION

You'll need at least 35 percent of your group's members to volunteer consistently in order to keep the organization active and sustainable.

—John Towle

hobbies

SNUG AFRICAN VIOLETS

African violets need small pots. As a rule, the pot should be one third the width of the plant; for example, a six-inch plant needs a two-inch pot.

—Mary Ellen Parker

food and drink

Leave Some Foods Behind

At the grocery store, never take the last of anything. There's probably a reason no one else bought it.

—Rulesofthumb.org Review Board

computers and technology

THE COST OF MOBILITY

A laptop will tend to be two thirds as powerful and one and a half times as expensive as a desktop with similar features from the same manufacturer.

—Rulesofthumb.org Review Board

---

recreational vehicles

WHEN TO SHIFT GEARS

If your bicycle's gear is too high, your legs will tire before your lungs do. If the gear is too low, your lungs will tire first.

—John S. Allen, author

weather and temperature

GOING NUTS OVER WINTER

It will be a bad winter if squirrels build their nests low in the trees.

—Rodney Schabacker

writing and presentation

WRITING FOR THE GENERAL PUBLIC When providing directions, write at a seventh-grade-English level.

—Rulesofthumb.org Review Board

joker

MODERATE GOOD FORTUNE

You can have a hot job, a hot lover, or a hot apartment. But you can't have all three at the same time.

—Armistead Maupin, author

style and appearance

TYING ONE ON

It's more important for the color of a man's necktie to agree with the color of his shirt and trousers than with his jacket.

—Rulesofthumb.org Review Board

health and body

Gauging Chest Pain

If applying pressure with your fingers causes a change in chest pain, it is probably a muscular pain.

—Marilyn Rider

automobiles

Interpreting Backfire

If a gasoline engine backfires through the carburetor, the mixture is too lean. If it backfires through the tailpipe, it is too rich.

—Rulesofthumb.org Review Board

pets

CHOOSING A POOCH

If a dog tolerates gentle handling between its toes, it's probably well suited for children.

—from the Pets Are Wonderful Council

house and home

FINDING A STUD

If you need to locate a stud in a stick-framed wall, keep in mind that most electricians are right-handed. Find an outlet and tap the wall directly to its left to find the stud. You can measure away from it in 16-inch increments to find the others.

—Art McAfee

advertising and design

AD (OVER)-EXPOSURE

The more often an ad is seen, the more effective it is, regardless of how dull or uncreative it may be.

—Rulesofthumb.org Review Board

sports and recreation

BUYING HOCKEY SKATES

The size of your skate should be approximately one size smaller than your shoe for men, and two sizes smaller for women. Your toenail should just about touch the front of the toe box and your heel shouldn't lift up in the back as you walk.

—Joy Veronneau

wild card

DIGGING YOUR OWN GRAVE

When digging a grave by hand, haul away 17 wheelbarrow-loads of dirt and pile the rest by the hole. You will have just the right amount to backfill.

—Randall Lacey

gambling

BETTING ON A BUTT Bet on the horse with the highest butt.

—Russell T. Johnson

food and drink

THAT BLOCK OF PEAS

Avoid buying bags of frozen vegetables that are in a solid lump; they've probably thawed and been refrozen.

—R. A. Heindl

relationships and romance

ROBBING THE CRADLE

If you want to date someone younger, find out what age is socially acceptable by using the following formula: your age divided by 2, plus 7. For example, if you are 26, then $26 \div 2 = 13 + 7 = 20$.

—Thomas Powell, environmental scientist

the arts

The Rock Band Roadie Rule

If you are in a four-piece rock band, plan on spending about eight hours total to pack up your equipment, travel to your local gig, unload, set up, play one set, break down, load up, and return home. Add an extra half hour for each additional instrument and one full hour for each additional set played.

—Mark McMullen

health and body

Clammy Hands

If you are too busy to use hot-air hand dryers in public restrooms, your lifestyle is too hectic for your health.

—Gerald Gutlipp, mathematician

pets

A SHINING STEED

A horse with a dull coat needs more corn in its diet.

—George Huebner

construction and architecture

ERGONOMIC BLACKSMITHING

Adjust the height of your anvil to match the bottom of your natural hammer stroke.

—Dennis Williams, blacksmith

food and drink

AGING A LOBSTER

Estimate the age of a large lobster by multiplying its weight, in pounds, by seven.

—Rulesofthumb.org Review Board

safety and survival

LEANING A LADDER

To check a ladder for proper lean, stand straight with your toes against the ladder beam and your arms straight out. If your hands fall on a rung in a comfortable grasping position, the ladder is set properly for climbing. If only the fingertips touch, the ladder is too far from the building; if the heel of the hand touches, the ladder is too close.

—from the National Fire Protection Association

business and sales

OPENING AN ELECTRONICS REPAIR SHOP

An electronics repair shop will require a population of 50,000 to support it.

—Tom McNamee

career and work life

GRILLING DRILLS

Interview first for the jobs you care about least—the experience will improve your performance at the important interviews.

—John Munschauer, author of *Jobs for English Majors and Other Smart People*

writing and presentation

BLOG IT 'TIL YOU MAKE IT

You need to post more than once a week to have any hope of attracting readers to your blog. Daily postings are even better.

—Rulesofthumb.org Review Board

sports and recreation

HANGING UP A ROPE

A climbing rope is overdue for retirement when you can no longer feel the separate strands while your hand slides along it.

—Peggy Kerber, editor of *Mountaineering*

relationships and romance

YULETIDE TALLY You should receive at least two Christmas cards for every three you mail out. If you don't, you are sending cards to the wrong people.

—Shelley Mosher

math and measurements

The Greenback Ruler

U.S. paper currency is about six inches long. (Denomination is unimportant.)

—Rulesofthumb.org Review Board

hobbies

APPRAISING CRYSTAL ANTIQUES

The lower the lead content on a crystal bowl or goblet, the clearer the "ping" will be when it is tapped.

—Wendy Ksiow

construction and architecture

A STEP ABOVE THE REST

When designing stairs, keep in mind that an incline of 38 to 42 degrees is most comfortable, and people shouldn't have to climb more than 18 steps before they reach a landing.

—Robin Berghuijs, architect

automobiles

PERFECT INDOOR PARKING

When nosing your car to a wall, turn on your high beams and look at the reflection on the wall as you slowly move closer. When the brightest part falls out of view, you are close enough.

—Jon Roppolo

green living

Sustainable Lighting

Compact fluorescent lightbulbs (CFLs) use about one third the energy of a regular incandescent. If you replace three frequently used lightbulbs with CFL bulbs, you will save $60 in electricity costs and reduce carbon dioxide emissions by 300 pounds per year.

—Rulesofthumb.org Review Board

children and child care

SNOWSUITING YOUR KIDS

Up to when children are six years old, you can determine their size by doubling their age.

—L. Musselman, mother

animals and wildlife
SHOOTING DUCKS
It is usually safe to assume that if you are missing shots at crossing ducks (ones flying by left to right, or vice versa), you are shooting behind them.

—Nelson Bryant

house and home
ENCROACHING ROACHES
Roaches never travel alone. If you caught one, expect there to be more.

—Richard S. Patterson, entomologist

conversation and body language
Thwarting Optimism
If you ask a negative question, you will get a negative answer.

—Denis Smith, high school counselor

math and measurements

THE ROMAN ARMY MILE If you're marching in step and marking the times the left foot strikes the ground, a mile will be 1,000 drumbeats.

—Gary Wheeler

health and body

Cigarette Abstinence

If you don't start smoking before age 25, you're unlikely to ever start.

—Rulesofthumb.org Review Board

wild card

DATING A WATERWAY

The more curves in a river, the older it is.

—Paul A. Delaney

children and child care

SCREENING FOR SCHOOL

When universal education was introduced in the Philippine Islands, there were no birth records and sorting children by age was a problem. The teachers determined that a child is old enough to send to school when she can cross her arms over her head and grasp her ears with her opposite hands. (This tested age-dependent body proportions as well as the ability to follow directions.)

—Arma L. Curtis

sports and recreation

FLY FISHING FOR TROUT

If you don't get a strike after seven casts, move on to the next likely spot on the stream.

—Sheridan Anderson, author of *The Curtis Creek Manifesto*

cooking and entertaining

STICK IT UP

When spaghetti is done, a strand will stick to the wall.

—Rulesofthumb.org Review Board

safety and survival

POLAR COOKING

The more arctic an animal's habitat, the greater the danger in eating its liver.

—Gerry M. Flick, ship's surgeon

food and drink

SCRIMPING ON VODKA

Running cheap vodka through a Brita filter four times will make it just as smooth as the good stuff.

—Rulesofthumb.org Review Board

science

Evolutionary Road

Organisms do not return to an ancestral condition or completely lose the effects of an ancestral condition. A species, for instance, won't evolve backward, but you can usually tell what it has evolved from.

—John J. Chiment, paleobiologist and editor

the arts

TIME TO MOVE ON

When panning across a scene in a movie, allow at least five seconds for an object entering one side of the screen to pass out the other side.

—Christopher Wordsworth, filmmaker

weather and temperature

SQUEAKING STEPS

If snow squeaks when you walk on it, the temperature is ten degrees Fahrenheit or less.

—Rulesofthumb.org Review Board

cooking and entertaining

FEELING THE HEAT

Your fire is ready when the charcoal is light gray. Test the heat by placing your hand, palm side down, three inches over the grill grate and counting the seconds you can hold it there. Twelve to fifteen seconds indicates a low-temperature fire; six to seven seconds, medium temperature; and one to three seconds, high temperature.

—Carolyn Flournoy

money and finance

Keeping a Friend

Never loan a friend more than you can afford to give away.

—Reed Alvord

pets

FEEDING FRENZY If your pet fish do not
consume their food within five minutes, you
have fed them too much.

—Rick Broadhead, aquarium hobbyist

automobiles

SHOPPING SMART FOR USED PARTS

A used car part should cost no more than 60 percent of the new part list price. However, a used mechanical or electrical part should go for half the rebuilt price and one quarter of the new one.

—LeRoi Smith, car builder

fitness and exercise

TRIPLE PLAY

Calculate the maximum distance you should run in a race by multiplying the average distance you run daily by three.

—Rulesofthumb.org Review Board

style and appearance

INSPECTING SPECTACLES

Put on glasses and look at your feet. If the glasses start to slip down your nose, they're too loose.

—Paul Lampe

food and drink

COOKING A HEALTHFUL CASSEROLE

You can double the veggies and halve the meat without doing any harm to the flavor of a casserole.

—Rulesofthumb.org Review Board

house and home

The Dope on Soap

Fifty percent of the amount of laundry detergent recommended by the manufacturer is plenty. This rule also applies to toothpaste.

—Mary Streit

wild card

LATE NIGHT FIRES

When the lights are on after 6 P.M. in the personnel department of a Silicon Valley company, look for layoffs within two weeks.

—Ben Cota, technology marketing guy

conversation and body language

The Spy Who Watched Me

If you think you are being watched, position yourself so the suspect is in sight and then look at your wristwatch. The suspected watcher will most likely look at his or hers as well.

—Rulesofthumb.org Review Board

joker

GUILT BY COMMISSION VS. OMISSION

Catholics feel guilty for what they weren't supposed to do and did. Jews feel guilty for what they were supposed to do and didn't.

—Michael Rider, graphic designer and art director

hobbies

CHUCKING WOOD

One person, working alone, can cut, haul, and stack about a cord of firewood a day.

—John Fay

construction and architecture

CONCRETE PLANS FOR THE DAY It takes one person the better part of a day to mix and pour two cubic yards of concrete.

—Ken Kern, writer and builder

education and school

IN A CLASS OF THEIR OWN

When giving instructions to a high school class, assume that three students will follow them incorrectly.

—David T. Russell, retired high school teacher

law and crime

SPOTTING A PESKY CLIENT

Never take a case if the prospective client arrives with more paperwork than you can read in less than five minutes.

—Rulesofthumb.org Review Board

travel

TURNING WARMER

The more often you make turns, the closer you are to your destination.

—James Parker, structural engineer

sports and recreation

BLOWING BUBBLES

One cup of laundry detergent per gallon of water makes spectacular soap for blowing bubbles.

—Rulesofthumb.org Review Board

business and sales

FLUFFING UP YOUR FIRM

A company's sales and marketing budget should equal at least 10 percent of its revenue.

—Elliot Miller

conversation and body language

SPEAKING UP

If you think that something goes without saying, it is probably in the best interest of everyone involved to just say it.

—William Krieger, English department chairman

wild card

Survey Shortcuts

To save time filling out a survey with rankings ranging from 1 to 5, don't waste effort deciding whether to put down a 1 or a 2, or a 4 or a 5, because these respective numbers are typically lumped together.

—R. A. Heindl

gambling

TOSSING THE DICE

If you need to roll a certain number with a pair of dice, take the difference between the number you want and 7, and subtract the result from 6. This will tell you how many chances in 12 you have of winning. For instance, if you need to roll a 9, the difference from 7 is 2. Subtract 2 from 6 and voilà! You have 4 chances in 12 of throwing a 9.

—Rulesofthumb.org Review Board

health and body

HEADS OR TAILS RESUSCITATION

If the face is red, raise the head. If the face is pale, raise the tail.

—Kate Gladstone

computers and technology

MONITORS AT A GLANCE

To protect your eyes from strain, make sure the screen is just beyond arm's length.

—Rulesofthumb.org Review Board

food and drink

JUDGING A WINERY

A winery's standards start to slip when it produces more than 50,000 cases annually.

—Richard Graff, chairman and COO of Chalone, Inc.

computers and technology

WORKING WITH MP3 FILES

Figure about 1 megabyte per minute to determine how much you can record on a device in MP3 format.

—Charles Shapiro

business and sales

BANKROLLING A NEW BUSINESS Don't start
a new business unless you can wait at
least one year before seeing a profit.

—Thomas O. Marsh

house and home

ROUND TABLE DISCUSSIONS

A rectangular table is most efficient, but a round table is more friendly. On the other hand, round tables take up more space and their linens are more costly.

—Rulesofthumb.org Review Board

gambling

DECIDING WHEN TO BLUFF

The higher the stakes, the easier it is to bluff.

—Edwin Silberstang, games expert

cooking and entertaining

Hosting the Kids

The number of guests at a child's birthday party should be limited to the age of the child. Invite three for a three-year-old, five for a five-year-old.

—Diane Gerhart

animals and wildlife
The Whale Scale
To estimate the weight of a gray whale, figure one ton per foot of length.

—Rulesofthumb.org Review Board

writing and presentation
A NOVEL APPROACH
To decide if you want to read an unsolicited novel, read one random page from the first third, one from the middle third, and one from the final third. If all three interest you, go back to the beginning and start reading. But if the book doesn't grab you in the first 30 pages, it never will.

—Gerard Van der Leun, editor and writer

children and child care
JUVENILE "RELINQUENCE"
Child-support payments for one child will usually equal 20 percent of the gross income of the parent who doesn't have custody.

—Carol Benjamin

joker

THE *MIDNIGHT EXPRESS* WARNING

If the water and food in a country are suspect, take similar precautions with the law.

—Rulesofthumb.org Review Board

the arts

AWARDS SEASON

A movie should be released after September to have a reasonable shot at winning an Oscar nomination.

—Pam Rahn, office Oscar pool winner

hobbies

THE PHOTO FILTER RULE

Any filter will lighten objects of its own color and darken those of a complementary hue.

—Paul Lisseck

green living

PRICING PRODUCTS

People will pay, on average, a 20 to 25 percent premium for products that are ecofriendly.

—Nathan Odle, civil engineer

weather and temperature

CAUGHT IN THE RAIN

If it starts to rain and llamas run for shelter, it's going to be a short storm. If they stay where they are, it's going to rain for a while.

—Dale Graham

safety and survival

A Silent Charging Dog

If a dog is charging you and barking, it is merely defending territory and will not bite. But a dog that's charging and not barking is going to attack.

—Rulesofthumb.org Review Board

career and work life

REDUCING YOUR PERSONAL BACKLOG Make a new "to do" list every day from your larger list of projects, goals, and things to do. If something gets transferred to the next day's list ten times, drop it. There's a reason you're avoiding the task.

—Rulesofthumb.org Review Board

advertising and design

Blanket Coverage

Run a TV commercial at least four times a day, four days a week, three weeks a month. If you run it less than that, your ad money would be better spent elsewhere.

—Scott Parker, data specialist

pets

SWAPPING CAT FOOD

When introducing a new food, allow three days for the cat to pout before you decide to try a different food.

—Rulesofthumb.org Review Board

house and home

RED LIGHT DISTRICT

Avoid buying a house within sight of a traffic light.

—Jim Colby

money and finance

CLIPPING COUPONS, OR NOT

If a coupon is worth less than a dollar, it's not worth clipping, sorting, and storing.

—Rulesofthumb.org Review Board

safety and survival

KNOT HALF AS MUCH

If you are using a rope with a knot or a sharp bend, assume that its strength is reduced by 50 percent.

—Frank Potts

style and appearance

DRESSING FOR THE STAGE

Always dress better than your expected audience. If they will be wearing jeans, for example, you should be wearing a suit; if they're in business attire, then wear a tux.

—Timothy Wenk, magician

automobiles

COMPARING ENGINES

Turbocharged cars (those that use an exhaust-driven turbine to maintain air-intake pressure) get about 10 percent better overall miles per gallon than regular cars of the same size and horsepower.

—Lawrence A. Howe, mechanical engineer

health and body

HEART-CONSCIOUS DRINKING

To lower your chances of developing heart disease, have one—and only one—alcoholic drink a day.

—Rulesofthumb.org Review Board

construction and architecture

Nailing It

Choose a nail that's two and a half to three times longer than the thickness of the piece of wood you want to nail.

—Alan H. Haeberle

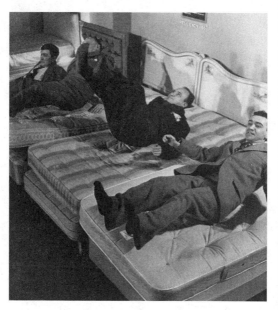

house and home

CHOOSING A MATTRESS The greater the back problem, the harder your mattress should be. The unforgiving surface forces you to move often so your muscles won't become stiff from lack of movement.

—Alan T. Whittemore, YMCA Physical Director

relationships and romance

Love at First Fidget

When first meeting a girl, watch what she does with her hands. If she plays with her hair, she likes you. However, if she rubs her nose, you don't stand a chance.

—Rulesofthumb.org Review Board

joker

BALLSY BESTSELLERS

The sales success of a sports book is inversely proportional to the size of the ball used in the sport.

—George Plimpton, writer and editor

cooking and entertaining

BOBBING FOR DRUMSTICKS

When deep-frying chicken in a commercial deep fryer, the chicken is cooked when a leg floats to the top.

—Tony Campo Jr., food service equipment salesman

money and finance

PERSONAL HEDGE FUND

Always have six months' salary in savings for emergencies.

—Rulesofthumb.org Review Board

health and body

RECOVERING ON PAPER

If you're fully insured, you will spend the equivalent of two full days doing insurance paperwork to cover seven days in the hospital.

—John E. Harney

math and measurements

DIVIDING BY THREE

A number is divisible by 3 if the sum of its digits is divisible by 3. For example: 1,326 is 1 + 3 + 2 + 6 = 12, and 12 divided by 3 = 4. Thus, 1,326 is divisible by 3.

—Catherine O'Doul

safety and survival

SKIRTING HIGH VOLTAGES

When you are in the vicinity of high voltage, keep 1 foot of distance between you and the power source for each 1,000 volts. For instance, stay 13 feet away from a 13,000-volt power source.

—Bob Crews, design scientist

food and drink

PRIX FIXED

The total meal should cost about two times the price of the entrées.

—Richard Patching

business and sales

Assigning a Task

Never ask someone to do something without including a specific time limit within which to complete the task.

—Rulesofthumb.org Review Board

animals and wildlife

Tracking a Deer

If deer droppings are black, moist, and glossy, they were left about 15 or 20 minutes ago and the deer is in the immediate vicinity. If the droppings are no longer glossy, then the deer is far away, probably bedded down on a southern slope.

—Sigmund Sameth

sports and recreation

PLANTING A PARASOL

To keep your beach umbrella from blowing away, bury one third of its handle in the sand.

—Joseph Liberkowski, ex-lifeguard

politics

THE PARTY IN POWER

If more than 40 percent of the likely voters have a favorable impression of an incumbent six months before an election, then he or she is probably unbeatable.

—Tom Wilbur, county commissioner

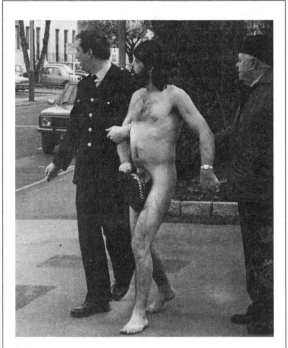

joker

TOTALITARIAN ATTIRE The more that local police uniforms resemble military uniforms, the less liberal and democratic that country is likely to be.

—Sam Roggeveen, editor of www.lowyinterpreter.org

hobbies

LEGROOM FOR LANDSCAPES

Assume the roots of normally shaped trees extend at least to the drip line of the branches.

—Shelly Wade, tree specialist

the arts

PLUCKING AT GUITAR STRINGS

The first string that breaks on a guitar is usually the high E (first string); the next strings likely to break are D and G (third and fourth).

—Ellen Klaver, musician

computers and technology

SPOILING YOUR EARS

One third of iPod buyers purchase a new pair of headphones within 90 days of buying the iPod.

—Chris Lyons, audio company product manager

pets

CARRY ON

A dog can comfortably carry half its weight in a backpack. Working dogs can carry up to twice their body weight for short periods.

—Alwyn T. Perrin, editor of *Explorers Ltd. Source Book*

conversation and body language

THE MARK OF A NARC

While talking to someone, a cop will be looking all around instead of directly at the person. He or she is not being rude, just observant. This is a good tip-off for spotting an undercover cop.

—Rulesofthumb.org Review Board

sports and recreation

The Power Launch

In bobsled competition, every second lost at the start costs three seconds at the finish. On a luge run, the time lost at the start is multiplied by four at the finish.

—attributed to an ABC TV Winter Olympics commentator

writing and presentation

STORYTELLING PRECISION

If you can't fit the idea of your story into one simple sentence, you don't understand your story.

—Craig Moorhead, writer

---

automobiles

CONFRONTING SPEED BUMPS

If the speed bumps are only a few inches in height, you'll feel them less if you speed up rather than slow down.

—Jerry Azzaro

green living

Toilet Blues

A leak from your toilet tank into the bowl can waste hundreds of gallons of water. To check for a leak, put three drops of food coloring in the tank and wait a half hour. If the color appears in the bowl, it's time to replace the tank's flapper valve.

—Jack Romig, green writer

the arts

MASKING MUSICAL MISTAKES If you're playing improvised music and flub a note or phrase in a scale, repeat the mistake to cover your tracks. Repeating it twice is even better.

—John Hornor Jacobs, creative director and musician

wild card

WAITING FOR DOCTORS

Expect to wait at least half an hour when you go to the doctor or dentist unless you get the first appointment of the day or the one right after lunch.

—Rulesofthumb.org Review Board

health and body

HOT TUB OVERFLOW

Soaking in a hot tub adds two to three pints of perspiration per hour per person to the water.

—Phil Tomlinson, woodworker

business and sales

WORKERS BY THE NUMBERS

As a manager, expect 80 percent of your work to be done by 20 percent of your staff. Also, expect 90 percent of your headaches/problems to come from 10 percent of your staff.

—Waldo Weyeris, engineer

children and child care

CONCEALING THINGS

If you're hiding something from a child, never hide it below your eye level.

—Jeff Brown

automobiles

MONITORING TIRE PRESSURE

Car tires will generally lose one pound of pressure for every 10 degrees Fahrenheit drop in temperature.

—Rulesofthumb.org Review Board

safety and survival

Awaiting a Tow

While waiting for roadside assistance, you need to stand to the side of your vehicle, at least one car length away. If the only place to stand is in front of or behind your vehicle, it is safer to stay in your car with your seat belt buckled.

—Donna Migliore, data analyst

wild card

Dialing for Dollars

The listener response to a radio call-in contest depends on the size of the prize being offered. Expect one call-in contestant for every dollar being given away.

—Don Burley, radio talk show host

joker

ACQUIRING BAD TASTE

Cheap beer is good beer, free beer is great beer.

—Dan O'Brien, grad student

sports and recreation

DEFENSIVE SCRABBLE

Always assume the other player holds a tile necessary to connect from your last move to a high score opportunity.

—Rulesofthumb.org Review Board

construction and architecture

AMPLE ELECTRICITY

To quickly estimate the amp load of a circuit, figure one amp per fixture or bulb.

—Ray Barbkenecht

science

STAR TRICK

While looking at the night sky with your binoculars, pick an object and watch it closely while you rotate the large end of the binoculars in a small circle. If you see a solid circle of light, it's a planet. If you see a broken circle, it's a star.

—Don Mattox

food and drink

PICKING A PEAR

A pear is ripe when the flesh near the stem yields slightly to thumb pressure.

—Gladys Sherwood

safety and survival

PROPER GUN HANDLING Never point an
unloaded gun at somebody.

—Rulesofthumb.org Review Board

cooking and entertaining

THE VANILLA CAP RULE

Most vanilla bottle caps will hold approximately one teaspoon, which is often the amount called for in baking recipes.

—Shelly Garrity

fitness and exercise

EXERCISING RESTRAINT

Never increase your training by more than 10 percent a week. Increases of 10 to 15 percent every three weeks make more sense.

—Rulesofthumb.org Review Board

advertising and design

A Designer's Worth

Freelance artists and graphic designers should determine their hourly rate by dividing their annual basic living expenses by 1,000.

—Michael Rider, graphic designer and art director

science

How High in the Sky

You can describe the location of objects that are low in the sky by holding your hand in front of you at arm's length, with your palm facing in and your pinkie on the horizon. The width of your hand covers 15 degrees of arc above the horizon.

—Hugh Crowell

cooking and entertaining

Food for Safe Keeping

Foods that are normally hard are bad if they've turned soft. Foods that are normally soft are bad when they've turned hard.

—Herman N. Cohen

money and finance

SAVING FOR RETIREMENT

By age 30 you should aim to be saving and investing at least 10 percent of your income for retirement.

—Rulesofthumb.org Review Board

sports and recreation

FITTING A FACE MASK

A face mask for skin diving or snorkeling fits properly if you can hold it on your face, out of the water, with nothing but the suction from your nose.

—Dorothy Hooker

law and crime

Doorway Robbery

Sitting next to the door on a subway will make you the easiest target for a purse snatcher or robber.

—Rulesofthumb.org Review Board

house and home

PUTTING OFF REPAIRS

The urge to fix up a new house is always strongest during the first 30 days. The longer you wait, the less apt you are to make the repairs.

—Eric Kimple

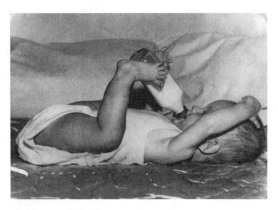

children and child care

THE ILLUSION OF AUTONOMY When giving a child a choice between two options, make sure both options are acceptable to you.

—Rulesofthumb.org Review Board

hobbies

BUYING ART FOR LESS

At auctions, paintings sell for half the price they go for in galleries.

—Richard Merkin, painter

business and sales

HALTING THE RUMOR MILL

If you don't want to start an office rumor, don't say anything you wouldn't write in a memo.

—Nancy Humphries, personnel consultant

education and school

Educated Guessing

If you're taking a multiple-choice test and you don't know the correct answer to a question, eliminate any answer that includes the words "always" or "never," choose the longest answer, and/or choose B or C because test makers avoid A and D.

—Rulesofthumb.org Review Board

food and drink

The Food Consigliere

To find good restaurants in a new town, ask the local butcher. He knows who buys the best cuts.

—from *Travelore Reports*

health and body

AS LONG AS YOU ARE WIDE

The distance between your fingertips, when your arms are outstretched at shoulder height, is equal to your height.

—C. Dees

weather and temperature

DETERMINING WIND DIRECTION

If you are flying over a rural area and need to know the wind direction at ground level, look at the cows. They normally stand with their heads downwind.

—Elaine Gibbons

animals and wildlife
DODGING A RATTLESNAKE

When determining the safe distance from a rattlesnake, figure that it can strike two thirds the distance of its length. In other words, a three-foot snake can strike two feet.

—Rulesofthumb.org Review Board

safety and survival
AVOIDING AVALANCHES

A snowfall of one inch or more per hour indicates a very high avalanche potential.

—Scott M. Kruse, biogeographer

the arts
TRIPPING ON TYPOS

Cheap paperback novels average one typographical error for every ten pages.

—Joe Applegate, typo hunter

money and finance

BANKRUPTCY BASICS

Don't consider bankruptcy unless you need more than five years to pay off your bills and high-interest consumer debt. Even then, consult a financial adviser to see if there's a better option.

—Greg Snyder

pets

CONFUSED CAT CALLS

When a cat becomes senile, it yowls as a way to orient itself.

—Franklin Crawford, writer

green living

Increasing Gas Mileage

Radial tires will get two to three miles per gallon more than bias-belted or bias-ply tires.

—Rulesofthumb.org Review Board

automobiles

INSURING AN AGING CAR Drop full coverage on your vehicle when it is five years old or reaches 75,000 miles.

—Ken Craig, auto mechanic

weather and temperature
Rocky Forecasts
Raccoons feed heavily 48 hours before the approach of a large winter storm.

—Thomas W. Neumann, anthropological
archaeologist and wildlife ecologist

*relationships
and romance*
HOLDING A GRUDGE
When someone says "I forgive you but I can't forget it," he or she probably has not forgiven you.

—Mark Soczek,
Ph.D., professor
at Michigan Tech
University

joker
A QUIET DINNER
The age of your youngest child in months is about equal to the duration of uninterrupted dinner conversation in seconds.

—Rulesofthumb.org Review Board

writing and presentation
Proofreading Statistics
Always expect to find at least one error when you proofread your own statistics. If you don't, you are probably making the same mistake twice.

—Cheryl A. Russell, editorial director of
New Strategist Publications

math and measurements
ESTIMATING HEIGHT
To determine the height (in feet) of a slope, throw a rock out level from the top of the slope and time its fall to the bottom. Square the number of seconds it takes the object to land, then multiply by 16. This will be your height in feet above where the rock landed.

—Rulesofthumb.org Review Board

business and sales
RUNNING A PROMO
The response rate for mass promotions through handouts, fliers, or cards is 2 in 1,000, or 0.2 percent.

—Dorian Kracht

sports and recreation

BEARING DOWN ON A GOALIE

A "2 on 0" is when two players attack the offensive zone with no one between them and the goalie. If you are going in on the goalie 2 on 0 and your partner passes the puck across in front of the net, shoot high because the goalie will be sliding across the bottom of the net.

—Joy Veronneau

career and work life

HIRE HOPES

If the interviewer talked more than you did, then the interview went well.

—David Shinn

automobiles

Built for Speed

Substitute lightweight aluminum for steel whenever possible. When working with aluminum, figure one third the weight and three times the cost of steel.

—Joe Ottati, car builder

health and body

SHOULDERING A LOAD For a short interval, you can lift twice your weight. For a long distance, you can carry half your weight uncomfortably or one fourth your weight comfortably.

—J. Baldwin, designer and writer

construction and architecture

Maintaining Your Edge

Plan on spending half an hour of maintenance for every two hours of chainsaw use.

—Rob Weinberg

style and appearance

MATCH POINT

If it doesn't match anything you own, don't buy it. It will never match anything you own.

—Stacy London, fashion expert for The Learning Channel

hobbies

MAKING CANDLES

One pound of wax will make eight 8-inch candles.

—Nancy Heffernan Eckstrom

house and home

WATERING YOUR LAWN

When dew is still on the grass, walk across your lawn; the impressions from your feet should last only several seconds. If it takes longer for the grass to spring back, then your lawn needs more water.

—James T. Dulley

computers and technology

HALF-BAKED EQUIPMENT

A computer can withstand temperatures up to 250 degrees Fahrenheit and still be salvageable.

—Rulesofthumb.org Review Board

food and drink

BROWN-BAG BEVERAGES

The cheaper the booze, the worse the hangover.

—Norman Evans

fitness and exercise

JUMPING ABILITY

The distance from the heel to the base of the calf muscle is an indication of jumping ability. For high-jumping dancers and athletes, the distance should be equal to or greater than the length of the foot.

—Stephanie Judy

health and body

Frozen Stiff

Hypothermia victims are not dead until they're warm and dead.

—Richard Wolkomir

hobbies

PHOTO FRACTIONS

When shooting a landscape photo, mentally divide the photo horizontally into thirds. Shoot so the horizon sits on the line above the bottom third.

—Rulesofthumb.org Review Board

children and child care

Passing Through

If a breast-feeding baby thoroughly wets his or her diapers at least six times a day, the baby is getting enough liquids.

— Rulesofthumb.org Review Board

travel

THE TRAVELING RULE OF TWO

Take twice the money and half the clothes you think you will need.

—Betsy Wackernagel

automobiles

LISTENING TO A CAR'S NEEDS

When your car makes an unusual sound, the lower the pitch, the more likely it is to be something serious.

—Bill George

style and appearance

APPLYING THE RIGHT AMOUNT OF PERFUME Spray three squirts into the air and walk through the area in which you sprayed it.

—Barb Heil

business and sales

THE RESTAURANT RULE OF THREE

The third restaurant to go into a space is generally the one that succeeds.

—Jeff Furman, business consultant and
cofounder of Ben & Jerry's

sports and recreation

BOWING TO PRESSURE

A novice archer should be able to hold a bow fully drawn for 10 seconds without his or her arm shaking. An experienced archer should be able to hold a bow at full draw for 15 or 20 seconds before starting to shake.

—Cliff Burns, bow hunter

joker

THROWING A LOW BLOW

Any cop will tell you that in a bar fight, the shorter of the two men probably started it.

—Douglas H. Hanbury

automobiles

BACKWARD STEERING

When backing up a vehicle with a trailer, turn the bottom of the steering wheel in the direction you want the trailer to go.

—Roger Damon

cooking and entertaining

Making Cottage Cheese

A gallon of milk will make about a pound of cottage cheese.

—Rulesofthumb.org Review Board

green living

SOLAR HEATING

On a sunny day in most U.S. latitudes, one square foot of solar water-heating panel can heat about two gallons of water per day.

—Phil Tomlinson, woodworker

house and home

Buying High Quality

With clothing or rugs, the more threads per inch, the more durable the fabric will be.

—Rulesofthumb.org Review Board

food and drink

A FEAST FIT FOR A KING

Plan on one and a half pounds of king crab legs per person. Two pounds will serve two to three people if you're serving with additional entrées. If you're serving a room full of crustacean enthusiasts, plan on five pounds for every three people.

—Richard Gehring, mechanic and crab lover

relationships and romance

IS IT A GUY THING?

It is easier to get forgiveness than it is to get permission.

—Jerrell Roy

joker

PLANNING A CRIME

Find out when the police change shifts in the neighborhood. You can expect 25 minutes with no patrols, starting with the last 15 minutes of the shift that's ending. During this time, police officers are usually writing up reports and talking to the incoming officers.

—Sheridan Chaney

money and finance

BUYER BEWARE

In general, half the things at a garage sale are underpriced, while a quarter are probably overpriced.

—George Perfect, antiques dealer

advertising and design

FROM "YOUTUBE" TO "YOU GO, GIRL!"

The success of an online video marketing campaign is based 50 percent on actual content, 15 percent on the title, 20 percent on the little thumbnail image of the video, and 15 percent on promotion of the whole package.

—Siobhan Tyrrell, digital marketer

career and work life

BECOMING THE POPE Though any Roman Catholic male is theoretically eligible to become pope, your chances of getting picked are nil unless you make cardinal first. That cuts the potential competition from half a million to less than 200.

—John Wertenbach, pope watcher

pets

DOG GAZING

Your dog will behave better if you do not look it in the eye too often. The lead dog of a pack rarely does this, and your dog will feel more secure if it knows you are the leader. Look at your dog mostly when he is not looking at you.

—Rulesofthumb.org Review Board

sports and recreation

Weighting Your Diving Belt

Always position weights on a diver's weight belt so it's heavier in the front half. This will keep the release buckle from shifting behind your back during a dive.

—Dennis W. Bellingham

weather and temperature

SONGBIRD DOO-WOP

The warm weather of spring has finally arrived when the chickadees change their cry from "chick a dee dee dee" to "dee dee."

—Ronald and Christine Newberry

animals and wildlife

Expecting Piggies

When a sow conceives, make a notch at about the moon on your fingernail. When this mark grows off the end of the nail, the sow is about to give birth.

—Doug Webb

conversation and body language

REFLECTING AFFECTION

You know someone likes you if you look into his or her eyes and see the pupils dilate.

—Rulesofthumb.org Review Board

education and school

TIMING YOUR LESSONS

The most successful teaching lessons last 22 minutes, the exact length of the average TV sitcom.

—Steven M. Keisman, high school resource coordinator

business and sales
HAWKING THINGS TO KIDS

When marketing to kids, remember that children think they are five years older than they actually are.

—Rulesofthumb.org Review Board

joker
TRAVELING WITH TWO-PLY

The softer the currency, the harder the toilet paper.

—John Fountain

health and body
BEER BELLY BASICS

The first step is to measure the circumferences of the waist and hips. If the waist-to-hips ratio is over 1.0 in men or above 0.8 in women, the risk of heart attack or stroke is five to ten times greater than if the ratio is less.

—from *U.S. Pharmacist*

wild card

CRACKING A SECRET CODE If the high-frequency letters (E, T, O, A, N, I, R, S, H) occur very often, you can assume that you are dealing with a transposition cipher in which the letters remain the same but are rearranged in a new pattern. On the other hand, the repeated appearance of low-frequency letters indicates that a message has been written in a substitution code.

—John Laffin, cryptologist

safety and survival

ORIENTING NORTH

The bark on a dead tree holds moisture on the northern side. For this reason, the tree is usually wet under the bark on that side, whereas the other side is dry.

—Rulesofthumb.org Review Board

health and body

A Gut Feeling It's Busted

If you feel nauseated after injuring an arm or leg, you've probably fractured it.

—J. L. McClenahan

wild card

RAZOR-SHARP EDGES

Test the edge of a knife by touching it to the hairs on your forearm after sharpening. A knife is as sharp as it can possibly be if the hairs actually seem to pop when touched.

—D. Petzel, editor for *Mechanix Illustrated*

sports and recreation

The Hiker's Philosophy

Never step on what you can step over. Never step over what you can walk around.

—Dave Bull

style and appearance

SIZING A MAN'S JACKET

A dress jacket is the correct length if the hem reaches the tip of the thumbs when the arms are relaxed.

—Danny Speer

safety and survival

THE SURVIVAL RULE OF FIFTY

You have a 50 percent chance of surviving for 50 minutes in 50-degree water.

—Rick Eckstrom, structural engineer

cooking and entertaining

TOO MUCH OF A GOOD THING

You can add seasonings to what you're cooking, but you cannot take them out. So always start with half the amount of seasonings called for and taste before adding more.

—Viki Anderson

hobbies

PLANTING BY THE MOON

Plant root crops at the full moon. Plant above-ground crops at the new moon.

—Larry Beck

house and home

MAINTAINING YOUR WATER HEATER

If you have trouble remembering to check your water heater for corrosion or moisture, place something you use once or twice a year next to it, such as a drain plunger. When you have to use the plunger, give the heater a once-over.

—Rulesofthumb.org Review Board

business and sales

SNIFFING FOR SNOOPS

Checking an office for phone taps and electronic bugging devices takes at least four hours for each 5,000 square feet of office space (two hours for a sweep using electronic instruments and two hours for a physical search).

—from *Boardroom Reports*

recreational vehicles

CLOCKING AIR TIME

Fly at least 100 hours a year to stay proficient as a fair-weather pilot. If you're flying on instruments, make that 200 hours a year.

—Jack Barclay, flight instructor

safety and survival

Fleeing a Bear

Bears can outrun, outclimb, and outswim a human. Your only chance is to run downhill; the bear's center of gravity makes it difficult for it to follow.

—Rulesofthumb.org Review Board

fitness and exercise

KEEPING ON KEEPING ON If you can follow
a fitness program for 21 consecutive days,
you can follow it for life.

—Kenneth Blanchard, author

sports and recreation

Limp Dinghy

Never buy an inflatable boat under ten feet long; it's cheaply made.

—Rulesofthumb.org Review Board

the arts

BALANCING A BATON

You should be able to balance a good conductor's baton 1¼ inches up the shaft from the handle. If it balances any farther up the shaft than that, you'll hold the baton incorrectly to compensate, and your arm will get tired.

—Wendy Ksiow

children and child care

BANDAGE TO BOO-BOO RATIO

Figure on one box of 20 Band-Aids per child per month.

—L. Musselman, mother

money and finance

SHOPPING ON eBAY

Purchases on eBay average 30 percent less than retail.

—Rulesofthumb.org Review Board

math and measurements

VISUALIZING AN ACRE

An acre is about the size of a football field without the end zones.

—Kevin Williams

safety and survival

SURVIVING A PARACHUTE MALFUNCTION

If your main parachute only opens partway and you're trying to decide whether to use your emergency chute, which might tangle with the main chute and make things even worse, spit. If your spit goes up, use your emergency chute. If your spit goes down, your rate of descent is survivable.

—Ernst Luposchainsky III

joker

THE TALKING METER

If a taxi driver talks a lot, let him; if he doesn't talk, don't ask him to; and if he laughs all the time, never ask him why.

—Mark McMullen

fitness and exercise

EXERCISE RULES OF THREE

You have to exercise at least three times a week. If you leave more than three days between exercise sessions, gains will be canceled out. It takes about three weeks for your body to adjust to a new level of exercise.

—Ned Frederick, writer

food and drink

The Frozen Entrée Test

The quality of food at a restaurant is inversely proportional to the size of the restaurant's freezer.

—John Soranno, restaurant owner

recreational vehicles

DISSUADING BICYCLE THIEVES If using a U-lock, put the crossbar of the lock next to the frame and the U part around the object to which you're locking the bike. With enough leverage, thieves can pry open U-locks, but they risk rendering the bike useless when the lock is in this position.

—Rulesofthumb.org Review Board

construction and architecture

THE SQUARE DEAL

An odd-angled wall will cost twice as much as a wall built with 90-degree corners.

—Rick Eckstrom, structural engineer

automobiles

COLLECTING CARS

The first year and the last year of a classic car series are the most valuable.

—Rulesofthumb.org Review Board

health and body

EARLY TO BED

Each hour of sleep before midnight is equal to two hours of sleep after midnight.

—Nick O'Conner

hobbies

LIGHTENING UP THE MOOD

When you're shooting portraits, your brightest light should come from the side and above the face, casting a triangular highlight on the far cheek.

—Tom Nelson, photographer

house and home

PLUG AND PLAY

An extension cord should be as thick as the cord you plug into it.

—John Brink, building superintendent

construction and architecture

PLANTING A TELEPHONE POLE

One fifth of the length of a telephone pole should be planted below ground.

—Ron Bean

business and sales
THE GADGET FACTORY RULE
The materials for a mass-produced electronic device should cost about 10 percent of the retail price of the finished product.

—Ray Bruman

green living
REDUCING YOUR PAPER TRAIL
Using 100 percent recycled paper saves five pounds of carbon dioxide per ream over regular paper.

—Rulesofthumb.org Review Board

cooking and entertaining
Digital Rice
To cook rice, rest the tip of your index finger on top of the rice and add enough water to reach the first joint. This works for any size pot.

—E. Mankin

wild card

Pick Your Own Pocket

It takes almost twice as long to find something in your coat pockets when you are not wearing your coat, especially if you're in a hurry. If you have a flight jacket or parka with more than four pockets, you can save time by putting it on just to look through the pockets.

—Gerald Gutlipp, mathematician

sports and recreation

BREEZY CATCH

A wind from the south blows a hook in the mouth.

—Chet Meyers and Al Lindner, fishing experts

law and crime

AVOIDING JURY DUTY

To avoid being picked for jury duty, read a book. Many lawyers won't select jurors who are reading because they might be too independent.

—Rulesofthumb.org Review Board

conversation and body language

LOST CONNECTION If you lose your train of thought while on the phone, hang up. Your thought will return and you can redial. The other person will assume you were disconnected.

—Terry Larimore, therapist

sports and recreation

COUNTING ON KINDLING

One stick can't burn, two sticks won't burn, three sticks might burn, four sticks will burn, and five sticks make a nice fire.

—Gail Smith

weather and temperature

PREDICTING A FROST

When the temperature falls below 50 degrees Fahrenheit at sunset, watch for morning frost.

—Tim Matson

food and drink

THE SUSHI TEMPERATURE RULE

For best texture and flavor, raw seafood should be approximately room temperature when it reaches your table.

—Zane Latta, waiter/bartender

style and appearance

SOLE SURVIVORS

If you switch back and forth among three pairs of shoes, they will last as long as five pairs worn sequentially.

—Joe Cosentini, shoe store owner

safety and survival

DRIVING IN FREEZING RAIN

When driving in freezing rain, crack your window slightly to listen for the sound of water splashing from the tires. When the splashing ceases, the road conditions have changed to ice.

—Rulesofthumb.org Review Board

health and body

Hallucinating

If someone is experiencing auditory hallucinations, the diagnosis is usually mental illness. If someone is experiencing hallucinations involving sight, smell, or touch, the diagnosis is usually a physical illness.

—Gerry M. Flick, ship's surgeon

the arts

Scoring a Good Book

To find interesting and popular books in a library, look for the shelf where returned books are stored before they are reshelved.

—Andy Steinberg

house and home

COST PER STROKE

There is nothing more expensive than a cheap paintbrush. The added coverage you'll get from a fine brush will easily make up the difference in cost after the first gallon of paint.

—Maitlen W. Montmarency, painter

advertising and design

HOOKING YOUR AUDIENCE

To attract women, show babies and women in an advertisement. To attract men, show men.

—David Ogilvy, advertising expert and cofounder of The Ogilvy and Mather Agency

joker

BUYING THE KNOT The more money people spend on a wedding, the fewer years the marriage will last. The presence of ice sculptures at the reception is almost always fatal to the future of a marriage.

—Bruno Colapietro, matrimonial lawyer

the arts

PLAYING THE BIG APPLE

In order to play New York City bars, your band needs 45 minutes of original music.

—Rulesofthumb.org Review Board

education and school

SIMPLE MATH

If you can't explain a mathematical theorem to a ten-year-old, you don't understand it yourself.

—G. S. Tahim, mathematician

hobbies

ANTIQUES HAGGLING

When asking for a discount in an antiques or vintage store, remember that the standard discount is 10 percent. If that isn't enough for you, don't bother asking. There is no magic password to get you 50 percent off.

—Elle Greene

recreational vehicles

CROTCH WATCH

A bicycle's crossbar should come to your crotch when you straddle the frame with your shoes off and your feet flat on the ground.

—Leslie Warren

business and sales

SIMMERING DISCONTENT

For every complaint a company receives, there are 26 other customers with problems they're not bothering to report, and six of these are serious.

—Rulesofthumb.org Review Board

cooking and entertaining

Chicken Briquettes

To barbecue chicken for a large group of people, you'll need one pound of charcoal per whole chicken.

—John Van Der Mark, city fireman

wild card

Got Silk?

It takes 110 cocoons to make a tie, 630 to make a blouse. A heavy silk kimono equals the work of 3,000 silkworms that have eaten 135 pounds of mulberry leaves.

—Nina Hyde, writer for *National Geographic*

sports and recreation

PLACING A SHOT ON THE GREEN

Aim for a spot on the green that is one third of the way to the hole. Bounce the ball there and let it roll the other two thirds.

—Rich Armstrong, coach and golf strategist

gambling

A SAFE BET

If you're playing cards in any gambling game for over 20 minutes and have not figured out who the patsy at the table is, it's you.

—Rulesofthumb.org Review Board

food and drink

PREPARING A MENU

If you are bringing in food for a company or group, expect 10 percent of the crowd to be vegetarians or people who would prefer vegetarian food.

—Rulesofthumb.org Review Board

construction and architecture

CONSTRUCTIVE DICKERING

A typical profit for a general contractor, after material and labor markup, is 25 percent. Use this to your advantage when negotiating. During slow times, contractors may accept as little as 10 percent profit.

—Nathan Odle, real estate developer and civil engineer

pets

SPOTTING A BIRD DOG

In a litter of retriever puppies, those that carry objects around are the best bets.

—Larry Mueller, hunting dogs editor for *Outdoor Life Magazine*

travel

DROMEDARY DISTANCES A camel is good for 1,000 to 2,000 miles.

—Ned Gillette, adventurer

computers and technology

AMPED UP

The amps on a large sound system are the last things you should turn on and the first things you should turn off to avoid blowing out your sound system.

—DJ Drue, Club Casualty

automobiles

PASSIVE-AGGRESSIVE DRIVING

The heavier the traffic, the less you gain by changing lanes.

—Rulesofthumb.org Review Board

conversation and body language

Anchoring the News

It takes about one minute to read 15 double-spaced typewritten lines on the air, or about four seconds per line.

—Charles Osgood, CBS news commentator

business and sales

Front-Loading Your Fees

When dealing with a client who is frequently negligent with payments, charge twice as much as the job will actually cost, and then get half the money up front.

—John A. Van Doren

style and appearance

Telling Navy Blue from Black

If you have to ask yourself "Is it navy or black?" then it's navy. There's no mistaking black.

—Don Mattox

house and home

FREEZED OUT

If your key won't fit into a frozen lock, try sticking it in the snow for a few minutes. The metal will contract enough to unlock the door.

—Rulesofthumb.org Review Board

writing and presentation

THINK BIG ON A SMALL SCALE

A clear idea should fit on the back of a business card.

—Morris Cooper

health and body

THE "WINTER WOMAN" RULE

If you're relocating to northern New England, you can expect to gain about ten pounds in the winter.

—Rulesofthumb.org Review Board

math and measurements

PENNY SMART

It takes 4,500 pennies to fill a one-gallon container.

—A. R. Wadum

travel

MULE TRAIN MUNCHIES

When using horses and mules as mountain pack animals, you'll need to feed each one three quarts of grain every morning and night and ten pounds of hay per day.

—Martha Betcher

money and finance

Spotting a Recession

A recession occurs when the economy shrinks in two consecutive quarters (that's six months straight).

—Rulesofthumb.org Review Board

fitness and exercise

GETTING BACK INTO IT

Recovering an unused physical skill takes one month for each year of layoff.

—Norman Brenner

children and child care

UNADORNED DAUGHTERS Tell your teenage daughter to lay out the jewelry she wants to wear, then have her put away one third of the items. For makeup, she should lay out everything, then put away all but two items.

—Tim Hoff, concerned father

the arts

Rolling the Credits

Movie credits and subtitles should appear on the screen long enough to be read three times.

—Jim Maas, filmmaker

health and body

THE RIGHT CRUTCH

A crutch is the right height if you can fit three fingers between the top of the crutch and your armpit.

—C. A. Fuller, EMT

automobiles

STOPPING TOO CLOSE FOR COMFORT

If you can't see the license plate of the car in front of you at a stoplight, you're too close.

—James Vincent, driving instructor

cooking and entertaining
APPORTIONING 'TATERS
You can count on people eating twice as many potatoes mashed as they would baked.

—Ned Bounds

sports and recreation
FIELDING A POP FLY
When a pop fly is hit in an outfielder's direction, he or she should step back. (It's easier to make up ground running forward than running backward.)

—Rulesofthumb.org Review Board

food and drink
COMES WITH OWN BOWL
If a turtle covers the bottom of a five-gallon bucket, it will make a decent meal.

—Wayne Jennings

safety and survival

DON'T TAKE THE FAST TRAIN

Never try to hop a train that is moving faster than three seconds per standard car length.

—Gary Wheeler

animals and wildlife

Snake Comfort

A snake needs a cage with a perimeter equal to or greater than its body length.

—Rulesofthumb.org Review Board

politics

ROOM FOR ERROR

Reported error margins in polls and surveys are always underestimated. Multiply the reported margin of error by 1.7 to obtain a more accurate estimate.

—from the American Statistical Association

·324·

conversation and body language

EYE CONTACT SPORTS Two people who stare into each other's eyes for 60 seconds straight will soon either be fighting or making love.

—Pierce Butler

wild card

Judging Your Juggling

If you can do 20 consecutive throws of a new juggling act without a hitch, you're ready to perform it in front of an audience.

—Todd Strong, circus school student

food and drink

AN EYE ON FRESHNESS

To determine if a fish is fresh, check its eyes; they should be clean, bulging, shiny, and bright.

—from *The Frugal Gourmet*

house and home

CLOSET ALLOTMENTS

A woman with three times as many clothes as a man only needs twice as much hanging space; men's clothes take up more space per hanger.

—Rulesofthumb.org Review Board

green living

SHEDDING LIGHT ON ENERGY BILLS

Lighting will take up 30 percent of the overall power usage for a building.

—Rulesofthumb.org Review Board

pets

HOUSING HOMING PIGEONS

The inside of a pigeon loft should be low enough that a pigeon can't fly over your head and small enough that you can touch all four walls while standing in the middle.

—Dr. Herbert R. Axelrod,
retired pigeon racer

animals and wildlife

JUDGING A HORSE BY ITS HOOVES

When buying a horse, keep in mind: If its feet are no good, other virtues will be wasted.

—Gene Wolfe

sports and recreation
Taking a Hike
To estimate your hiking time, figure one hour for every three miles plus an additional hour for every 2,000-foot increase in elevation.

—Kevin Kelly, writer and technologist

food and drink
FINE WINING
Keep white wine in your fridge and take it out 30 minutes before serving. Keep red wine *out* of the fridge and put it in 15 minutes before serving.

—Mary Welch

house and home
PURRFECTLY COMFORTABLE
If cats aren't sleeping on the radiators, turn down the heat.

—Rob Shapiro

construction and architecture
Raising the Roof
A good roofer can finish 100 square feet an hour.

—Paul Polce, Ponzi's Antiques

automobiles
TRUE GRIT
Rub a little of your motor oil between your thumb and forefinger. If you feel any grit, it's time to change your oil.

—Donny Bates, gas station attendant

health and body
ABSORBING THE RIGHT CALCIUM
Place a calcium tablet in a few ounces of room-temperature vinegar and stir vigorously every 5 minutes. The tablet should disintegrate completely in 30 minutes or less. If it remains mostly intact after a half hour, chances are it won't be of any value to you.

—from *Consumer Reports*

animals and wildlife

SEPARATING THE SHEEP FROM THE GOATS
In general, sheep's tails hang down and
goats' tails stand up, though some breeds
of sheep look like goats and vice versa.

—Mary Ellen Parker

hobbies

CULLING YOUR SHOTS

The average photographer should expect to delete about 85 percent of the photos he or she shoots. If you want three good shots, you should plan on taking 20 to 25 pictures.

—Rulesofthumb.org Review Board

style and appearance

THE CINDERELLA RULE

You should have a thumb's width of space between your longest toe and the tip of your shoe.

—Charles J. Gudas, DPM, associate professor at the University of Chicago Medical Center

safety and survival

ESCAPING A RIPTIDE

Never swim against a riptide. Instead, swim at a 90-degree angle to it at an easy pace until you're clear of it. Then head back to shore.

—Jack Fleming

children and child care

PAINLESS LABOR

When trying to decide whether to get an epidural, keep this in mind: Unless you can slam your thumb with a hammer and not mind, get the epidural.

—Bobbie Wood, mother of three

business and sales

Hanging On for Sales

When taking an order over the phone, always let the customer hang up first. Jumping the gun can cut off a last-minute add-on.

—Rulesofthumb.org Review Board

cooking and entertaining

WRESTLING BREAD TO THE BOARD

Knead bread dough until your arms are tired and then do 25 more punches and rolls.

—J. Michaelson

computers and technology

In-Box Outbursts

When you check your e-mail and find yourself groaning "Ugh, this again?" it's time to create a filter.

—Merlin Mann, founder of 43folders.com

green living

PREVENTING LAZY LITTER

Most people will not walk more than 14 or 15 steps to throw away a piece of trash, so trash cans should be placed about every 25 paces.

—Rulesofthumb.org Review Board

career and work life

PURSUING A CONSULTING JOB

Personal contacts are best for getting consulting jobs. Twenty leads should produce one assignment.

—Dr. Jeffrey Lant

money and finance

LUNCH MONEY You'll get twice as much food for the same amount of money if you order the lunch combos from a Chinese take-out restaurant. Pick up a couple of lunch combos in the middle of the day, and take them home to feed the whole family.

—Rulesofthumb.org Review Board

weather and temperature

A BREAK IN THE WEATHER

If it is snowing and the tree trunks appear to darken at midday, the snow will change to rain.

—Rulesofthumb.org Review Board

advertising and design

OPTIMIZING YOUR BILLBOARD

People are exposed to outdoor advertisements for only a few seconds. So a good billboard should have no more than seven words and only two things to look at. And don't even think about putting a phone number unless it spells a simple phrase.

—Glen Lane

hobbies

LOPPING LIMBS

After pruning, use tree paint to cover all wounds that are larger than your thumbnail. It will protect the exposed wood until it heals.

—Shelly Wade, tree specialist

joker

THE ORIGINAL HITCHHIKING RULE

When hitchhiking, look like the person you want to pick you up.

—Stewart Brand, publisher of *The CoEvolution Quarterly*

business and sales

Waiting for a Sale

If no one stops the dog from barking within 15 seconds, they're not going to answer the door.

—Elaine Brooks, former Avon saleslady

recreational vehicles

DROPPING ANCHOR

Under normal conditions, use 7 feet of anchor line for every foot of water. If the water is 10 feet deep, you'll need 70 feet of anchor line.

—Peter Kim

money and finance

Housing Yourself

Your total monthly housing expenses, including your rent or mortgage, should not exceed 33 percent of your monthly income.

—Rulesofthumb.org Review Board

automobiles

RELAXED STEERING

Place your hands at the ten and two o'clock positions on the steering wheel. You should be close enough to make almost a full half-turn of the wheel without having to lean forward or have your elbows touch your body.

—Alan Johnson, SCCA national driving champion

the arts

THE POWER OF PATHOS

The best comic book villains don't know they're villains.

—Mark Andrew Smith, creator of *The Amazing Joy Buzzards*

conversation and body language

Spotting a Liar

If a person is recalling a real situation, his or her eyes tend to go up and left. You can assume the person is making up the story if his or her eyes go down and right.

—Rulesofthumb.org Review Board

politics

THE PERSONAL CONNECTION

Door-to-door canvassing, though expensive, yields the most votes. One additional vote is cast for every 14 people who are contacted.

—Alan B. Krueger

money and finance

BALANCING YOUR PORTFOLIO

The amount of your portfolio that should be invested in stocks depends on your age and should decrease as you get older. The conservative rule for finding the right percentage of stocks is to subtract your age from 100. A slightly more aggressive approach is to subtract your age from 120.

—Steve Flanders

writing and presentation

GET THE PICTURE? When speaking to
an audience, keep in mind that only 25
percent of people can effectively conjure
a visual image in their heads.

—Dr. Barbara Brown

business and sales

TRACKING ᴇBAY BIDDERS

When selling on eBay, expect 6 percent of your auctions to end in nonpayment by the winning bidder.

—Rulesofthumb.org Review Board

green living

MILITARY MILEAGE

Aircraft carriers get six inches to the gallon.

—Phillip Williams Jr.

computers and technology

SQUASHING SOFTWARE BUGS

The cost of fixing a serious software bug increases by ten with each phase of the development cycle. A $10 bug in the requirements phase will cost $100 to fix in the design stage, $1,000 to fix during development, $10,000 to fix during prerelease testing, and $100,000 to fix after it is released.

—Mike White, independent IT consultant

pets

Mare Care

Expect to spend at least one hour per day feeding and grooming a horse.

—Mary Flinn,
co-owner of
Starlane Farms

joker

MAKING AN IMPRESSION

People are more likely to remember you if you always wear the same outfit.

—Rulesofthumb.org Review Board

travel

MISSING BY A MILE

A one-degree error in course will take you about a mile off track for every 60 miles you travel.

—Dr. Bill Grierson, professor emeritus at
the University of Florida

business and sales

Keeping Meetings Short and Sweet

The better the agenda, the shorter the meeting. People will focus on the list and be more reluctant to stray when they have a set number of things to accomplish.

—S. L. Young, project manager

food and drink

Itsy-Bitsy Berry Season

When you find garden spiders in your raspberries, you have one week left to pick the fruit.

—Carol Ayer, raspberry grower

health and body

HUMAN HORSEPOWER

Working hard at physical labor or exercise, the average person can generate about one-quarter horsepower, which is roughly equal to the power output of a small model airplane engine.

—Rulesofthumb.org Review Board

pets

DOG TIME Anything over 45 minutes seems like forever to your dog. You'll be greeted as enthusiastically coming back from a two-hour shopping trip as you would coming back from a two-day vacation.

—Andrea Frankel

relationships and romance

BREAKING UP IS HARD TO DO . . . QUICKLY

Recovery time from a breakup is equal to the half-life of the relationship. For example, it takes about two and half years to fully recover from a five-year relationship.

—Bill Mayer

food and drink

The Beef over Surf and Turf

Steak restaurants serve good seafood, but seafood restaurants serve terrible steak.

—Rulesofthumb.org Review Board

health and body

THE HEART RULE

A healthy person's heart is about the size of his or her fist.

—Thomas O. Marsh

style and appearance

Wood in Shoes

Using cedar shoe trees will increase the life of your shoes by 50 percent. You only need one pair. Put them in soon after taking your shoes off. They will absorb moisture and help the shoes keep their shape.

—Rulesofthumb.org Review Board

cooking and entertaining

CARNIVOROUS PORTIONS

Plan for a quarter pound of boneless meat or a third to half pound of bone-in meat per person.

—Dan Whitlock

wild card

WAVE WATCHING

Every seventh wave is a big one.

—Annette Arthur

pets

COMPARING A DOG'S AGE TO A HUMAN'S

The old rule—multiplying a dog's age by 7 to find the equivalent human age—is incorrect. To calculate a dog's age in human terms, count the first year as 15, the second year as 10, and each year after that as 5.

—Pierce Butler

relationships and romance

THE HUGGING NEED

Four hugs a day are the minimum needed to meet a person's "skin hunger."

—Greg Risberg, clinical social worker

writing and presentation

DRAFTING A SPEECH

Professional speechwriters budget an hour and a half of research, thinking, and writing for every minute of speech.

—from *Canadian Business* magazine

style and appearance

SIZING YOUR HAT

If you can stick your thumb under the brim, it's too big.

—Glenn O'Brien, The Style Guy for *GQ*

sports and recreation

COMPATIBLE CAMPMATES

A camping trip is in jeopardy whenever early risers or night owls exceed 50 percent of the party. If either is a majority, the other campers should reassess their plans.

—Denis Smith, high school counselor

animals and wildlife

The Fifth Little Piggie

It takes the profit from four pigs to pay the cost of keeping a sow. The fifth pig is the first one that makes you money.

—Julius E. Nordby, author of *Swine*

construction and architecture

DOLING OUT OFFICE SPACE Provide 250 square feet of floor space for each vice president, 200 for middle managers, and 175 for clerks.

—Thomas Underhill, tech company owner

computers and technology

Buying a Hard Drive

Expect the actual capacity of a hard drive to be about 93 percent of its advertised capacity. For example, you'll be able to store about 112 gigabytes of data on a 120 gigabyte hard drive.

—Rulesofthumb.org Review Board

weather and temperature

PREDICTING RAIN

Ring around the moon, rain by noon. Ring around the sun, rain before the night is done.

—Joe Schroeder

safety and survival

DODGING A POLAR BEAR

If a polar bear charges you from behind, dodge to the right. Eskimos say most polar bears are left-pawed.

—L. M. Boyd

conversation and body language

A CHANGE OF HEART

When a person telling an emotional story slips from first person to third, he or she has reached the point where the feelings start to become overwhelming.

—Terry Larimore, therapist

business and sales

FAST-FADING FADS

You have 90 days to make and ship a novelty item and 90 days to sell it out. After that, inventory costs swallow up the profits.

—Fred Reinstein, fad merchant

food and drink

TAKING CARE OF THE BARTENDER

Tip your bartender at least a dollar a drink, even at an open bar. Increase the amount in a fancier place, in a big-city bar, or if you want more generous pours on your refills.

—Rulesofthumb.org Review Board

travel

CHOOSING THE RIGHT CAMEL

Don't choose a camel that trembles while sitting. This means its front legs are bad.

—Lauren Stockbower, photojournalist

money and finance

REFINANCING YOUR MORTGAGE

Consider refinancing your mortgage whenever you can lower your interest rate by two points or more.

—Rulesofthumb.org Review Board

recreational vehicles

Going Hog Wild

New motorcyclists get cocky and reckless when they've put 3,000 miles—or the equivalent of one trip across the United States—on their bikes.

—Wolfman, Hell's Angel

safety and survival

KEEPING A SAFE DISTANCE If the target is within range, so are you.

—Rulesofthumb.org Review Board

health and body

Getting a Grip on Portions

To estimate the amount of food you should eat in one sitting, clasp your hands together. The meal should be no bigger than your hands. If it is, you're eating more than your body needs.

—Rulesofthumb.org Review Board

fitness and exercise

FINDING YOUR COLLAPSE POINT

Your collapse point is about three times the average distance you swim, cycle, or run each day. For example, if you run an average of three miles a day, you should be able to run nine miles without stopping.

—Ken Young, statistician

sports and recreation

THE BALL IN THE ROUGH

To find a golf ball, first look ten yards past where you think you hit it out, then look ten yards short, and finally look five yards farther into the rough.

—Michael Miles

law and crime

ORDINANCE SUBORDINANCE

The amount of corruption in a society is directly proportional to the number of laws the society has.

—Jim Butler

house and home

Racing the Sun

Try to live east of where you work; the sun will always be at your back during your commute.

—Rulesofthumb.org Review Board

hobbies

CAUTIOUS ANTIQUING

A poorly lit and unkempt store is a reliable indicator of the quality of its offerings. The poor lighting and messiness help to hide imperfections and other surprises you'll find once you've left with a purchase.

—Elle Greene

education and school

RAISING YOUR HAND

When an instructor says "Please correct me if I made a mistake," do it once and only once.

—Rulesofthumb.org Review Board

wild card

Moving a Tree

The root-ball of a tree that is being moved should be ten times the diameter of the tree's trunk. So if the tree has a 5-inch trunk, the root-ball needs to be 50 inches in diameter to survive the move.

—Dr. George E. Fitzpatrick

business and sales

UNLOADING A COMPANY

The sale price of a small business should be between seven and ten times the average profit of its last three years in operation.

—Bill Chellberg

gambling

Picking a Good Slot Machine

Slot machines closest to the doors are the most generous. Bar slots pay better than the machines that show apples, oranges, and cherries. Machines with several slots, requiring more than one coin per pull, pay better.

—Rulesofthumb.org Review Board

weather and temperature

BUZZWORTHY FORECAST

If bees stay at the hive, expect rain. If they fly away, expect good weather.

—Mark Wysocki, meteorologist

automobiles

SPENDING FOR FENDER BENDING

The collision deductible for your car should equal one week's take-home pay.

—Robert Fair, insurance adjuster

business and sales

FIVE'S A CROWD The productivity of a meeting is inversely proportional to the size of the group when more than four people attend.

—Steven M. Keisman, high school resource coordinator

advertising and design

FLIPPING OVER ADS

A well-designed ad will look just as good upside down.

—Michele Rogers,
advertising creative director

food and drink

FREE-RANGE FATS

Beef fat tinged with yellow means an animal was grass fed; white fat means grain fed.

—Dennis Palaganas

safety and survival

AVOIDING LIGHTNING

During a lightning storm, if the hair on your arms and head starts to stand on end, lightning is going to strike in your immediate vicinity. Drop to your knees and bend forward, putting your hands on your knees. Don't place your hands on the ground, or you will be vulnerable to ground current if a lightning bolt hits within 50 yards.

—from the National Fire Protection
Association

law and crime

SPEEDING WITH CONFIDENCE

If you're speeding on a rural interstate, follow young men in pickups with local plates. They know where the speed traps are.

—Larry Gassan

wild card

STRUNG OUT

To untangle something, keep pulling the mess outward, making it larger and looser until the loops free themselves. This is your only hope of success.

—Rulesofthumb.org Review Board

science

HOT CHEMISTRY

In general, the rate of a chemical reaction doubles for every ten degree Celsius rise in temperature.

—Ken Partymiller, chemist

pets

Befriending a Frightened Mutt

A stray dog who is afraid of people will trust the people associated with the dogs it plays with.

—Andrea Frankel

animals and wildlife

Flipping a Bird

Most songbird eggs hatch in two weeks. The chicks then leave the nest two weeks after they hatch.

—Thomas Powell, environmental scientist

house and home

PACKING FOR A MOVE

Pack any item you'll use right away last. Your corkscrew, bottle opener, screwdriver, hammer, box cutter, and packing tape shouldn't be packed at all; these items go in a "don't let it out of your sight" bag.

—Rulesofthumb.org Review Board

automobiles

PHOTOGRAPHING A CAR A three-quarter front view makes the most effective photograph for selling a car.

—Paul Douglas, photographer

sports and recreation

ESTIMATING WALKING SPEED

To determine your walking speed (in miles per hour) with a three-foot stride, count the number of steps you take in two minutes and divide that number by 30.

—James V. Vaughter

writing and presentation

CHECKING IT TWICE

Two rounds of proofreading catch 98 percent of the errors in a book.

—Bill Kaupe, consultant

math and measurements

CONVERTING MILES TO KILOMETERS

To convert miles to kilometers in your head, double the number of miles four times and then divide by 10. And to convert kilometers to miles, halve the number four times and multiply by 10.

—Rulesofthumb.org Review Board

house and home

DROWNING IN JUNK MAIL

For every magazine, newspaper, or catalog you subscribe to, you will receive at least five pieces of junk mail per month.

—John Towle

health and body

SHIVERING TO WARM

Shivering produces as much heat as running at a slow pace, or roughly the amount of heat generated from eating two medium-size chocolate bars per hour.

—Peggy Kerber, editor for *Mountaineering*

conversation and body language

SHOUTING YOURSELF OUT

In Japan, the first person to raise his or her voice loses the argument.

—Cally Arthur, editor and communications coordinator

safety and survival

A Long Leash on a Short Fuse

Wait at least an hour before investigating a charge of dynamite that didn't go off.

—Joe Kaiser

the arts

SNAPPING GUITAR STRINGS

When you install new strings on a guitar and need to play right away, tune the guitar to pitch, grab each string at the twelfth fret, stretch it straight up off the fret board, and let it snap back down. Retune. Repeat twice, and the strings will hold their tune.

—Rulesofthumb.org Review Board

hobbies

DEEP SEA PHOTOS

Most leaks in an underwater camera show up at very shallow depths. If no leaks appear within 15 feet of the surface, there is a 95 percent chance that none will appear at greater depths.

—Flip Schulke, underwater photographer

health and body

Assessing Nerve Damage

Skin with damaged nerves doesn't wrinkle in warm water.

—Rulesofthumb.org Review Board

conversation and body language

LOST IN TRANSLATION

When conversing in your native language with people who don't speak it fluently, assume that they understand about half as much as they appear to understand.

—Stephen Cudhea,
English-language instructor

style and appearance

A FITTING CONCLUSION

Fit comes before fashion. If your clothes don't fit right, nothing else matters.

—Kim Kohler-
Lovejoy,
fashionista

relationships and romance

A FAMILY AFFAIR You don't just marry your spouse, but your spouse's entire family. Make sure you're ready to spend the rest of your life with them as well.

—Moses Moore

food and drink

THE PUNCH COUNT

When making an alcoholic punch, figure four weak, three strong, two sweet, one sour.

—Gordon Stewart

health and body

TRACKING FOOT PROBLEMS

A sneaker sole worn along the outer edge indicates flat feet. A sole worn along the inner edge indicates a high arch.

—Rulesofthumb.org Review Board

joker

Rank Optimism

The worse the men's room smells, the easier it will be to sell lottery tickets at the bar.

—Peter Leach

the arts

Critiquing Movie Reviews

Look at the names of the critics praising a movie in advertisements. If you've never heard of them, the movie isn't any good.

—David Malki, filmmaker and cartoonist

automobiles

RUNNING ON EMPTY

If your tank is on empty and you're trying to make it to the next gas station, cut your speed to 35 miles per hour.

—R. C. Woods

politics

"READING" YOUR CONSTITUENTS

Politicians attach a "weight" to comments from constituents. A form e-mail reflects the opinion of 5 people. A personal e-mail, fax, or postcard reflects the opinion of 10 people. A form letter reflects the opinion of 20 people. (This includes handwritten notes that are obviously part of an organized letter-writing event.) A phone call reflects the opinion of 30 people. A truly personal letter reflects the opinion of 50 people.

—Rulesofthumb.org Review Board

house and home

ON A ROLL

The average paint roller will apply two to three square feet of paint per dip.

—Rulesofthumb.org Review Board

health and body

DIY Obstetrics

Lay a cloth tape measure over the belly, pressing one end on the pubic bone. The number of centimeters from the pubic bone to the top of the uterus is the number of weeks of pregnancy.

—Dr. Ann Dorney

wild card

INCHING ALONG THE HIGHWAY

On rainy nights, 90 percent of the worms crossing a highway will be facing the same direction.

—Emery Nemethy

money and finance

YOUR FINANCIAL SAFETY NET

For a minimum level of financial security, your net worth (the cash value of all your assets) minus all your debts should equal one year's income.

—J. Snyder, credit manager

sports and recreation

LANDING A BLUEFISH

Troll your lure at five times the length of your boat.

—Bill Berger

automobiles

A RAPIDLY DEPRECIATING ASSET

No matter what you paid for your new car, as soon as you drive it off the dealer's lot its value immediately drops to the National Automobile Dealers Association wholesale price, which is the maximum amount the dealer would pay to buy it back.

—Rulesofthumb.org Review Board

cooking and entertaining

THREE-ALARM FRYER When a film of smoke begins to rise from the hot fat in the donut machine, it is the right temperature for frying donuts.

—Helen Ward

hobbies

Crossover Appeal

The carpenter's rule of thumb "measure twice, cut once" applies as well to sewing and knitting.

—Debbie Stoller, author of *Stitch 'n Bitch*

education and school

GUESSING WITH YOUR GUT

Never change your first guess on a multiple-choice question when checking over your answers. The first guess is always the best one.

—William H. Smith

business and sales

TOP SELLERS

The best salespeople aren't the ones with the most sales but the ones with the most reorders.

—Rulesofthumb.org Review Board

PLAYING THE OUTFIELD

A left-hander will hit to the right 85 percent of the time, so outfielders should shift to the right.

—Rulesofthumb.org Review Board

gambling

KNOWING WHEN TO FOLD 'EM

Call it a night after winning half of your session's stake. If you started out with $2,000, quit when you reach $3,000. You may ride out a hot streak, but as soon as you lose one bet, it's time to quit, convert your profits to traveler's checks, and mail them home.

—Marvin Karlins, Ph.D., author of
Psyching Out Vegas

cooking and entertaining

Using Dried Herbs

Use one third the amount of the dried herb as you would use fresh. For example, one teaspoon of dried crushed basil equals one tablespoon of fresh chopped basil.

—Marion Berger

green living

STAYING OUT OF HOT WATER

When looking to lower water-heating costs, keep in mind that showers account for two thirds of the bill.

—Rulesofthumb.org Review Board

the arts

SELLING SCI-FI

Science fiction books with green covers don't sell as well as those with blue covers.

—Sci-fi publisher

math and measurements

Finding the Depth of a Well

To find the depth of a well or open mine shaft, square the number of seconds a stone takes to reach the bottom and multiply by 16. If a stone takes 3 seconds to fall to the bottom of a shaft, then $3^2 = 9$, and $9 \times 16 = 144$ feet to the bottom.

—Joe Cleary

sports and recreation

TALL SWIMMERS FINISH FIRST The maximum speed for a human swimmer is one body length per second. For sprints, all other things being equal, the tall swimmer has a distinct advantage. This is derived from Froude's law, which says that as you increase the length of a watercraft (including the human body) at the waterline, the drag decreases.

—Steve Flanders

food and drink

Shopping the Perimeter

The most nutritious foods (vegetables, meats, breads) are located around the perimeter of the grocery store; the center aisles are used for low-nutrition, high-profit junk foods.

—Bill George

health and body

LISTENING TO YOUR BODY

If you don't know what you want, it's probably sleep.

—Timothy Wenk, magician

house and home

HEATING WITH PEOPLE

Ten people will raise the temperature of a medium-size room one degree per hour.

—John Brink, building superintendent

hobbies

THE GOOD GROUP PHOTO RULE

You have to take more than one photo of a group to get one without someone blinking. To calculate the number of shots needed, divide the number of people by 3 if there's good light and by 2 if the light's bad.

—Dr. Piers Barnes

safety and survival

PACKING A PISTOL

The handle of your holstered revolver should hang midway between your wrist and your elbow with your arm at your side.

—Alan Ladd, in the movie *Shane*

weather and temperature

THE COLD FACTS

To estimate the windchill factor, subtract the wind velocity from the temperature.

—Becky Ridgeway

house and home
AVOIDING WHITE ELEPHANTS

Never buy a kitchen appliance designed for only one kind of food (like a bagel toaster).

—Rulesofthumb.org Review Board

style and appearance
SQUEAKY HEEL

The louder the noise a pair of closed-toe women's shoes makes on a hard floor, the less comfortable the shoes.

—Arb Elbow

computers and technology
Making Easy Connections

If you are installing a new computer part, remember that you should never have to force equipment into the desired slot. A proper installation will quickly *snap* into the socket and feel secure. If a part is hard to insert into a slot on the motherboard, try rotating it to face the opposite direction.

—Rob Walker

wild card

PASSING THE TIME IN LINE

The number of minutes you will wait in line at the bank is equal to the number of people ahead of you divided by the number of tellers times 2.75.

—Chuck Davis, writer and broadcaster

animals and wildlife

NEUTERING TIME

Castrate a calf when his testicles are the size of a squirrel's head.

—Jim Crissman, veterinary pathologist

food and drink

SQUEEZING YOUR MUSSELS

Squeeze a mussel's shell together. If it doesn't stay shut, it's dead.

—Margaret Wagner

hobbies

A WELL-DRAWN FACE When drawing a portrait, keep the following in mind: The eyes are on a line halfway between the top of the head and the chin, with their inside corners one eye-width apart; the nose is almost halfway between the eyes and chin and is as wide as the distance between the eyes; the corners of the mouth fall directly below the pupils of the eyes; and position the ears so their tops are at eye level and their bottoms fall below the nose but above the mouth.

—Alex Stewart

automobiles

THE HANDS-FREE TIRE CHECK

If you think your front tire is low while driving, take your hands off the steering wheel. A low tire will cause the car to drift in the direction of the low tire.

—John H. Beauvais

business and sales

STAYING IN THE BLACK

A magazine or newspaper needs to be about 60 percent advertising to survive financially.

— John Schubert, senior editor

travel

MICKEY'S MOB

At Disney World, the crowd is most likely to turn to the right. Therefore, the rides to the left are less crowded.

—Carolyn Lloyd

the arts

FROM KUBRICK TO MICHAEL BAY

Purely as a guide, ten seconds is quite a long shot and three seconds is quite short.

—Christopher Wordsworth, filmmaker

food and drink

THE CIDER HOUSE RULE

A bushel of apples will make slightly more than three gallons of cider.

—Rulesofthumb.org Review Board

house and home

CARING FOR NEW WOODWORK

Rub linseed oil into new woodwork once a day for a week, once a week for a month, once a month for a year, and once a year from then on.

—Marilyn Rider

conversation and body language

Assessing Clout

You have social clout when you bore people and they think it's their fault.

—Will Musham, composer and writer

advertising and design

SETTING TO READABLE WIDTH

Avoid columns of text less than 35 characters per line, because shorter lines break up sentences, which makes them hard to understand. Also avoid columns of more than 65 characters per line, because they often force readers to read the same sentence more than once.

—Peter Smith, publication designer

law and crime

PREPARING FOR A DEPOSITION

Each hour of effective deposition in a civil action case requires three hours of preparation.

—Stephen Verbit, attorney

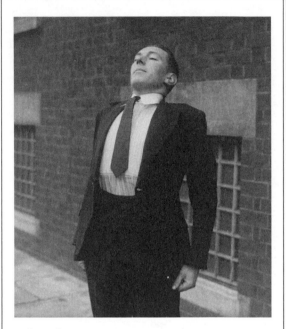

style and appearance

ADJUSTING A TIE A man's tie should reach the middle of his belt buckle.

—Thomas Powell, environmental scientist

pets
SETTING UP AN AQUARIUM
Provide at least one gallon of water for each inch of fish.

—Rulesofthumb.org Review Board

the arts
SHOOTING SUNSETS
The best window of time for photographing sunsets is about seven minutes before to seven minutes after the sun has set.

—Andrew Mullen

sports and recreation
WINNING MONOPOLY
The person who makes the most deals wins.

—Jennifer Evans

writing and presentation
CLEAR IDEAS
If your data has fewer than 20 pieces of information, a graphic presentation is not needed.

—Edward R. Tufte, author of *The Visual Display of Quantitative Information*

cooking and entertaining
BARBEQUE INFERNO
When preparing fatty foods, leave 40 percent of the grill exposed to avoid flare-ups caused by too much grease dripping down on the coals.

—Gerri Willis

safety and survival
Avoiding a Crash in a Car Race
Aim your vehicle for the spot where the car first spun out. At high speed, nothing stays in the same place for long. The car will have moved by the time you get there.

—Joie Chitwood, former Indy driver

sports and recreation

The Ski Lift Rule

For each minute of skiing downhill, plan on seven minutes riding on a ski lift.

—Rulesofthumb.org Review Board

science

SCHOOL OF SOFT KNOCKS

Don't tap the face of a sticky gauge or a fidgety dial on a piece of electronic equipment any harder than you would tap the bridge of your nose.

—Steve Parker, aerospace engineer

health and body

ESTIMATING YOUR RING SIZE

For men, ring size equals glove size equals shoe size.

—R. L. Liming

children and child care

INFANT INFLATION

A pediatrician's rule of thumb is that a healthy infant should roughly double his or her birth weight by six months of age and triple it by one year.

—Rulesofthumb.org Review Board

safety and survival

SPOTTING A WATER MOCCASIN

To tell a poisonous water moccasin from a harmless water snake, look at its eyes. A moccasin has elliptical pupils, like a cat's, whereas a water snake has round pupils.

—Thomas Pilette

sports and recreation

The Mountaneer's Wind Rule

A plume of snow blowing from a peak higher than 23,000 feet means a wind of at least 100 miles per hour at the summit.

—Dr. David Kumaki

recreational vehicles

GOING SOLO AS A STUDENT PILOT Once a
student pilot follows the basic safety rules
without exception and seven out of ten
landings are good ones, he or she is ready
for the first solo flight.

—Dale Scharpenberg, flight instructor

conversation and body language

MAPPING OUT PERSONAL SPACE

Americans stand just far enough apart when talking that, arms extended, they could insert their thumbs in each other's ears.

—Roger Axtell, author of *Do's and Taboos Around the World*

health and body

JOINT APPRAISALS

If the patient arrives at a hospital hopping on his or her good foot, the bad ankle is almost certainly not broken.

—Dr. Paul Trotman

sports and recreation

Footwear to Scale

According to the 1952 Everest Expedition, one pound added to your boots equals five pounds added to your back. Buy the lightest boots that are safe.

—David A. Lloyd-James

fitness and exercise

Stretching Your Muscles

You cannot stretch cold muscles. Warm up with mild exercises for at least five minutes beforehand or there are no gains from stretching.

—Rulesofthumb.org Review Board

safety and survival

ON THIN ICE

Check the thickness of the ice on your skating pond after you've had three consecutive nights of about 20 degrees Fahrenheit. If it's been warmer than that, your pond isn't safe to skate on. And remember that blue ice is safer than black ice.

—Joy Veronneau

joker

RULE OF THUMB RULE

A rule of thumb works four out of five times (including this one).

—Paul A. Delaney

ABOUT THE AUTHOR

Tom Parker is an author and illustrator, and also an IT project manager at Cornell University. He has written and illustrated *Rules of Thumb,* volumes 1 and 2; *In One Day;* and *Never Trust a Calm Dog.* His work has appeared in *The Wall Street Journal, Audubon, National Wildlife, Glamour,* and *The Whole Earth Catalog,* and he is currently a contributing writer for *MAKE* magazine. When Tom is not collecting rules of thumb, he is a flight instructor and flies a 1956 Cessna 180 bush plane.

PHOTO CREDITS

Cover *(clockwise from top right)*: Getty Images; Jupiter Images; Paul Taylor/Getty Images; Shutterstock

Jon Crispin: p. 165, 174, 192, 275, 380; **Getty Images:** Herman Agopian p. 133, Troy Aossey p. 65, Altrendo Images p. 289, Archive Holdings Inc p. 151, 352, 389, Archive Photos p. 371, Robin Bartholick p. 348, Joey Berg p. 106, Howard Berman p. 243, Tim Bieber p. 298, Marti Cale p. 234, Harry Cape p. 111, Greg Ceo p. 19, Steve Cole p. 24, Colorblind p. 5, Ralph Crane p. 33, D. De Boer p. 170, Carl De Souza p. 220, Loomis Dean p. 161, Nick Dolding p. 74, John Dominis p. 188, Evening Standard p. 56, Chip Forelli p. 361, Fox Photos p. 138, 279, 366, 375, General Photographic Agency p. 69, 197, Peter Ginter p. 142, Bob Gomel p. 115, Jan Greune p. 120, Charles Gullung p. 216, Sylvain Grandadam p. 101, Sumio Harada p. 97, Gideon Hart p. 202, GK Hart/Vikki Hart p. 51, Hill Street Studios p. 334, Dana Hoff p. 28, Hulton Archive p. 83, 179, Hulton Collection p. 257, 270, Sean Justice p. 293, Keystone p. 129, 238, 343, Quique Kierszenbaum p. 339, Romilly Lockyer p. 357, John Lund p. 124, Douglas Miller p. 261, Steve Murez p. 266, Kelvin Murray p. 156, 284, Donald Nausbaum p. 321, Nikolaevich p. 302, Karen Pearson p. 92, Potter p. 325, Andy Reynolds p. 147, Roberts p. 88, Simon Roberts p. 10, 311, David Samuel Robbins p. 183, Lisa M. Robinson p. 248, Frank Rothe p. 60, Gregg Segal p. 229, George Silk/Time & Life Pictures p. 252, Paul Taylor title page, Tom Till p. 207, Jason Todd p. 225, Travel Ink p. 316, UpperCut Images p. 79, William Vanderson/Hulton Archive p. 330, Weegee (Arthur Fellig) p. 14, Welles p. 384, Chaloner Woods p. 307, David Zaitz p. 42; **Dede Hatch:** p. 38, 211; **Jon Reis:** p. 47